JavaScript: Software Development (2025-2026 Edition)

Azhar ul Haque Sario

Copyright

First Printing, 2025

Azhar.sario@hotmail.co.uk

ORCID: https://orcid.org/0009-0004-8629-830X
LinkedIn: https://www.linkedin.com/in/azharulhaquesario/

Disclaimer: This book is free from AI use. The cover was designed in Microsoft PowerPoint.

Contents

Part 1: The Modern JavaScript Landscape (2025+)

Foundations of JavaScript Software Development

1.1. The JavaScript Ecosystem: From Browser Script to Global Standard

To write JavaScript in 2025 is to stand on the shoulders of giants and, at the same time, navigate a landscape that changes with dizzying speed. Understanding this ecosystem isn't just trivia; it's the single most important skill for staying relevant. We call this "Ecosystem Literacy."

The Evolution from Script to Standard

JavaScript's story begins in 1995. It was created in 10 days by Brendan Eich at Netscape, not to be a serious programming language, but to be a simple "scripting language" for web designers to add basic interactivity to static HTML pages. For a decade, it was widely seen as a toy, plagued by inconsistencies between browsers like Internet Explorer and Netscape Navigator.

The first great shift was standardization. To save the language from corporate warfare, it was submitted to

Ecma International, which now manages its official specification under the name ECMAScript. This is why you see JavaScript referred to as "ES6" or "ECMAScript 2025."

This specification isn't decided in a vacuum. It's evolved annually by TC39 (Technical Committee 39), a group of engineers from companies like Google, Apple, Microsoft, and PayPal. They follow a rigorous, public-facing, four-stage process to introduce new features. A feature, like 2025's Promise.try, begins as a "Stage 0: Strawman" (an idea) and must gain consensus, provide multiple implementations, and pass strict tests before it can reach "Stage 4: Finished" and become part of the official language.

The second, and arguably more profound, shift was the creation of the Google V8 engine in 2008. Before V8, JavaScript was interpreted, which is slow. V8 introduced high-performance JIT (Just-In-Time) compilation. When your code runs, V8's interpreter (named Ignition) starts executing it immediately. Behind the scenes, its optimizing compiler (named TurboFan) watches your code. If it sees a "hot" piece of code (like a function inside a loop), it performs on-the-fly type analysis, compiles that function into hyper-optimized machine code, and swaps it in. The result was a 10x performance leap that made complex web applications like Google Maps possible.

Finally, in 2009, engineer Ryan Dahl took the V8 engine, pulled it out of the browser, and connected it to operating system a-la-carte (like file systems and networking). He called this Node.js. This was the inflection point. Suddenly, JavaScript was no longer just a "frontend" language; it was a "backend" language. It became a dominant force for building fast, scalable servers, and the ecosystem exploded.

The 2025 Development Stack: npm, Vite, and the Tooling Shift

That explosion created the modern stack. The heart of this stack is npm (Node Package Manager), which is, without exaggeration, the largest software library in the world. It's a vast, public registry of free, open-source code "packages." Need to handle dates? npm install date-fns. Need to build a server? npm install express. This is the core principle of modern development: don't reinvent the wheel.

However, managing millions of packages created a new problem: "build tooling." In the 2010s, tools like Webpack became standard. Webpack's job was to take all your JavaScript files, all your CSS, your images, and your npm packages, and "bundle" them into a few static files the browser could understand. But on large projects, Webpack became a monster. It was complex, required arcane configuration, and build times could stretch to 5, 10, or even 30 minutes.

This is why, by 2025, the ecosystem has decisively shifted to next-generation tools like Vite. The difference is profound. Webpack bundles everything before you can even see your changes. Vite, by contrast, uses native browser features (ESM) to serve files on demand. When you start your app, it's instantaneous. When you change a file, only that one file is updated (Hot Module Replacement), and your browser refreshes in milliseconds. This isn't just a small speedup; it's a fundamental improvement to the "developer experience," allowing for a flow state that was impossible before.

Real-Time Case Study: The TypeScript Tsunami (2025)

The final, and most important, piece of the modern ecosystem is TypeScript. For years, JavaScript's greatest strength (its dynamic, flexible typing) was also its greatest weakness. In a large, multi-developer codebase, this flexibility leads to chaos. A function might expect a number, but you accidentally pass it a string, and the program only crashes at runtime, in front of a customer.

TypeScript, a superset of JavaScript, solves this. It adds a static type system that runs before the code ever executes. It's a "compiler" that checks your work, ensuring you're not making simple,-type-related errors.

This is no longer a preference; it is a non-negotiable enterprise standard. In a 2025 case study on its internal engineering practices, the observability platform Datadog detailed its large-scale migration to TypeScript. Their engineers stated that static typing was essential for "scalability and maintainability." When you have hundreds of developers working on a single product, the ability for the compiler to provide "early error detection" and for the code to be self-documenting (you can see what data a function expects) isn't a luxury. It's the only way to manage complexity and reduce business risk.

This is the skill of Ecosystem Literacy: The ability to articulate why the industry moved from Webpack to Vite (developer experience) and why it adopted TypeScript (maintainability and risk reduction). It's understanding that your tools are not just preferences, but solutions to concrete, expensive business problems.

1.2. The JavaScript Paradigm: A Multi-Paradigm Language

One of the most powerful and confusing things about JavaScript is that it doesn't force you into a single way of thinking. Unlike a pure language like Java (OOP) or Haskell (Functional), JavaScript is a multi-paradigm language. It provides a toolbox of different models, and the senior developer's job is to know which tool to use for which problem.

JavaScript rigorously supports three distinct models.

Event-Driven Programming: This is the foundational model for all interactivity in JavaScript. You don't write a program that runs from top to bottom; you write functions that react to events. A user clicks a button ('click' event). Data arrives from a server ('load' event). A timer finishes ('timeout' event). This is the basis of the browser's interactivity and, crucially, the core of Node.js's I/O model.

Object-Oriented Programming (OOP): JavaScript has a... complicated relationship with OOP. It has a native prototypal inheritance model, which is powerful but confusing to developers from a classical background. To make it more familiar, modern JavaScript (since ES6) introduced the class keyword. This is "syntactic sugar" over the old model, but it provides a clean, familiar way to encapsulate state and behavior.

Functional Programming (FP): This is the "secret weapon." It's what led programming luminary Douglas Crockford to call JavaScript "Lisp in C's clothing." This model is built on the concepts of first-class functions (a function is just a value, like a number or string, that you can pass around), closures (a function remembers the "world" it was created in), and immutability (not changing data, but creating new data from it).

Updated Application (2025): From Loops to Declarative UIs

For years, the functional side of JavaScript was ignored. But in the modern 2025 stack, it has become the dominant and most important paradigm for data transformation, especially when working with UI.

Imagine you have an array of user objects and you want to get a list of their names.

The "old," imperative way would be to use a for loop:

JavaScript

```
// Imperative (The "how")
let names = [];
for (let i = 0; i < users.length; i++) {
  names.push(users[i].name);
}
```

This code works, but it's low-level. You are manually creating an empty array, managing an index variable i, and mutating (changing) the names array on each loop.

The modern, functional way is to use a declarative array method:

JavaScript

```
// Declarative (The "what")
const names = users.map(user => user.name);
```

This single line is more than just shorter; it's a different way of thinking. You are not describing how to loop; you are describing what you want. You are "mapping" one set of values to another. This is cleaner, less error-prone (no i to get wrong), and it's immutable. The .map() method doesn't change the original users array; it returns a brand new names array.

This exact principle—using .map(), .filter() (to get a new array with some items), and .reduce() (to "boil down" an array to a single value)—is the foundational beating heart of a framework like React. A React component is just a function that takes state (data) and "maps" it to UI. When your state changes, React re-runs the function, creating a new, declarative description of the UI. This functional, declarative approach to managing data flow is the dominant principle of all modern web development.

Real-Time Case Study: Refactoring at Atlassian (2024)

The tangible impact of these principles isn't just "cleaner code"; it's a massive, measurable performance win. In 2024, the engineering team at Atlassian, makers of Jira and Confluence, published a case study on a large-scale refactor of their JavaScript codebase.

Their problem was a common "best practice" that had gone horribly wrong: the use of "barrel files." A barrel file is a single index.js file in a folder that re-exports all the other files in that folder. It seems convenient; you can import 10 components from one place.

But Atlassian discovered this was destroying their build performance. When a build tool like Webpack sees import { Button } from './components', it can't tell which of the 100 components in that barrel file you really need. This breaks "tree-shaking" (the process of removing unused code), forcing the bundler to include massive amounts of dead, unused code in the final application.

By applying modern functional principles (favoring explicit, direct imports) and writing a script to automatically refactor their entire codebase to remove barrel files, the Atlassian team achieved a staggering "75% faster build" time. This is a real-world, multi-million dollar win. It means developers aren't waiting 30 minutes for a build; they are shipping features faster, and the company is innovating more quickly.

This is Paradigm Fluency: the ability to look at a task and choose the right tool. You use OOP to encapsulate a complex service (class ApiService). You use Event-Driven patterns for I/O. And you use a Functional, declarative-first approach for all data transformation and state management.

1.3. Thinking in JavaScript: The Event Loop and Concurrency Model

If you take away only one concept from this entire chapter, make it this one. The JavaScript concurrency model is the single most misunderstood—and most powerful—part of the language.

Here is the central paradox: JavaScript is a single-threaded language.

This means it has one "Call Stack." It can only do one single thing at a time. If you have a task that takes 10 seconds, the entire application—all UI, all clicks, all scrolling—freezes for those 10 seconds. This is called "blocking the main thread."

This should make JavaScript a terrible language for the web. So how can it possibly handle thousands of user actions, multiple network requests, and complex animations all at once?

The answer is that the JavaScript engine itself is single-threaded, but the environment it lives in (the browser or Node.js) is not. JavaScript achieves its "concurrency" by offloading slow tasks to this environment and using a mechanism called the Event Loop to check on the results.

This model has four key parts:

The Call Stack: This is where work is done. When you call a function, it gets "pushed" onto the top of the stack. When it finishes, it gets "popped" off. It's a "Last-In, First-Out" (LIFO) system.

Browser/Node APIs: These are the "slow" parts that live outside of JavaScript's main thread. This includes things like setTimeout, fetch (for network requests), and any DOM event (like a click). When you call fetch('/api/data'), JavaScript doesn't wait. It hands that task over to the Browser's internal networking API and immediately moves on to the next line of code.

The Task Queues (Callback/Task & Microtask): When a slow task in the APIs is finished (e.g., the network data has arrived), it doesn't just interrupt the program. It places its "callback function" (the code that should run after the task is done) into a waiting area. There are actually two queues:

Macrotask Queue (or Task Queue): For "big" tasks like setTimeout, setInterval, and I/O.

Microtask Queue: For "small," high-priority tasks, primarily Promise.then() and async/await. This queue always gets to go first.

The Event Loop: This is the manager. It's a simple, endlessly-running loop that asks one question: "Is the Call

Stack empty?" If the stack is empty (meaning all synchronous code has finished), it checks the Microtask Queue. It will run every single thing in the Microtask Queue until it's empty. Then, and only then, will it check the Macrotask Queue and move one item from it to the Call Stack to be executed.

Updated Application (2025): Visualizing and Debugging Blockers

This isn't just academic theory; it's the core of all performance debugging. In 2025, your most critical skill is using browser and Node.js profiling tools (like the Chrome DevTools Performance tab) to visualize this process.

You will encounter a bug where a user clicks a button, and the UI freezes for two seconds before an animation plays. Using the profiler, you'll record a "flame graph" and see a giant, solid yellow block labeled "Scripting." This is your enemy: a long-running, synchronous task that is blocking the main thread.

Your job is to fix it. You'll identify that the "long-running task" is, for example, a complex calculation over a huge array. Using your knowledge of the Event Loop, you "fix" this by breaking the user's perception of time. You use setTimeout(yourFunction, 0).

This doesn't make the code faster. Instead, it tells the browser, "Take this heavy yourFunction and put it in the Macrotask Queue." The Call Stack becomes empty, the UI updates instantly (the button press is registered), and then, on the very next "tick" of the loop, your function is pulled from the queue and executed. The user perceives this as an instantaneous, responsive application.

Real-Time Case Study: Node.js at Slack (2025)

There is no better real-world example of the Event Loop's power than the architecture of Slack. Slack has to handle millions of concurrent users, all connected at the same time, sending messages, images, and notifications in real-time.

In a traditional, multi-threaded model (like Java or C#), the server would dedicate one system thread to each connected user. This is incredibly expensive. A thread consumes significant memory. Scaling this to millions of users would require a mind-boggling amount of hardware.

Slack is built on Node.js. Because of its event-driven, non-blocking I/O model, Node.js can handle millions of concurrent WebSocket connections on a single server. How?

When a user connects, Node.js doesn't create a new thread. It simply attaches an event listener (a callback function) to that connection. When a message comes in from user A, the Event Loop sees a new "I/O" event. It executes the tiny callback function, which might look up user B and send them the message. That "send" operation is also non-blocking. The function finishes, the Call Stack is empty, and Node.js is free to handle an event from a different user—all on the same single thread.

This architecture is only possible because of the Event Loop. It allows a single thread to efficiently juggle millions of "waiting" tasks, only spending CPU cycles on the active work that needs to be done right now. This is the skill of Performance Debugging: understanding that in JavaScript, performance is not about raw speed; it's about responsiveness and never, ever blocking the main thread.

1.4. The Development Environment: Tooling and Best Practices

Code is not written in a vacuum. The final pillar of our foundation is the professional "workbench"—the set of tools and processes that separates a hobbyist from an engineer. This is the curriculum taught in elite programs like MIT's Web Lab and Berkeley's CS169: software engineering is the process just as much as it is the product.

A professional developer is expected to be fluent in this workbench from day one. It's the baseline.

Necessary Knowledge: The Developer's "Workbench"

Version Control (Git): This is the non-negotiable standard. Git is the "save" button for your entire project, but more importantly, it's the "collaboration" button. It's a distributed system that allows hundreds of developers to work on the same code without overwriting each other's work. It's the safety net that lets you experiment, knowing you can always revert to a stable state.

IDE (VS Code): The Integrated Development Environment is your "workshop." While many exist, VS Code has won the developer mindshare. It's not just a text editor; it's a platform. Its power comes from its ecosystem of extensions, most critically ESLint (which analyzes your code for errors as you type) and Prettier (which automatically formats your code on save). This combination ends all team arguments about code style and catches countless bugs before they're even saved.

Command Line (CLI): The graphical user interface (GUI) is for using software. The command line is for building it. You must be comfortable in your terminal. It's how you'll run your tools (Vite, npm, Git), manage your server, and automate your workflow. Proficiency here is a mark of professionalism.

Browser DevTools: This is your diagnostic scanner and X-ray machine. You must have absolute mastery of the Console (for logging and debugging), the Elements tab (for inspecting HTML/CSS), and the Network tab (for watching every single request your application makes to a server).

Updated Application (2025): A "Vanilla-First" Setup with Vite

The 2025 trend is to get this workbench operational in seconds, with a "vanilla-first" approach. In the past, setting up a new project was a painful, multi-day process of configuring Webpack.

Today, we use Vite. From your command line, you will run a single command: npm create vite@latest.

This one command will ask you a few questions (like your project name and if you want to use TypeScript) and instantly scaffold a complete, professional development environment. You will then run npm install (to get your packages) and npm run dev (to start the server).

In under 30 seconds, you will have a blazing-fast development server running. When you open the project in VS Code, it will automatically suggest the recommended ESLint and Prettier extensions. Most importantly, it features near-instant Hot Module Replacement (HMR). You can have your app open on one screen and your code on another, and as you type, your changes appear in the browser instantly without the page even reloading.

This is a profound shift. It allows you to learn JavaScript and TypeScript first, without getting bogged down in a week of configuration hell. This is the 2025 "happy path" for all new development.

Real-Time Case Study: Google's "Build Your Technical Career" (2025)

Why do we emphasize this so much? Because it's what the world's best companies are hiring for.

In Google's ongoing campus outreach programs at universities like Stanford, their message is clear. They aren't just looking for "coders" who can solve an algorithm on a whiteboard. They are looking for engineers who understand the full software development lifecycle.
Their "Build Your Technical Career" events stress that modern software engineering is the tooling. It's Git workflow. It's automated testing. It's a CI/CD pipeline (Continuous Integration / Continuous Deployment) that automatically tests and deploys your code. Google is teaching students that mastery of this process is what they hire for, because that is what allows a company to scale. They value the engineer who can write a test and set up a build script just as much as the one who writes a clever algorithm, because they know that maintainable software is what builds an enterprise.
This provides you with the final foundational skill: a Professional Development Workflow. This is the baseline, day-one job requirement. It's the ability to use Git for source control (cloning a repo, creating a branch, making a commit, and opening a pull request) and to debug effectively within your IDE and browser.
With this foundation—Ecosystem Literacy, Paradigm Fluency, Performance Debugging, and a Professional Workflow—you are no longer just learning syntax. You are learning to be a software engineer.

The ECMAScript 2025 Standard and Language Internals

2.1. Core Language Features: Types, Coercion, and Modern Syntax

Welcome to the bedrock of modern JavaScript. To build complex, reliable applications in 2025, we must first have a rigorous, almost academic, understanding of the language's core. This isn't just about "making things work"; it's about knowing precisely why they work and, more importantly, why they sometimes break.

The Foundations: Primitives, Objects, and Equality

First, we must internalize the JavaScript type system. The language has a set of foundational "primitives." These are the simple, immutable building blocks: String, Number, BigInt (for math beyond the limits of Number), Boolean, Symbol (for unique identifiers), undefined (for unassigned values), and null (for intentionally absent values). Everything else is, in one way or another, an Object. Arrays are objects. Functions are objects. The new Temporal date-time objects are objects.

This distinction is critical. Primitives are passed by value; objects are passed by reference. But the most immediate challenge this system presents is "type coercion"—JavaScript's notorious habit of silently converting types. If you write 10 == '10', JavaScript sees two different types and tries to "help" by coercing the string '10' into the number 10, resulting in true.

This "help" is the source of countless bugs. In a 2025-ready curriculum, this behavior is not a feature; it's a legacy pitfall. This is why the "strict equality" operator (===) is non-negotiable. It checks both value and type, with no coercion. 10 === '10' is, correctly, false. This single practice is the first step toward writing predictable code.

We also build on a foundation of modern syntax. The var keyword, with its function-level scope, is a relic. We exclusively use let and const, which respect "block scoping" (they only exist within the {...} block they are defined in). This prevents variables from "leaking" out of loops or if statements. We also institutionalize destructuring and spread/rest operators as standard practice.

Legacy Code (pre-ES6):
JavaScript

```javascript
var config = { host: 'api.example.com', port: 443 };
var host = config.host;
var port = config.port;
console.log(host, port);
```

Modern Syntax (2025 Standard):
JavaScript

```javascript
const config = { host: 'api.example.com', port: 443 };
// Destructuring to extract values
const { host, port } = config;
console.log(host, port);

// Spread syntax to copy
const newConfig = { ...config, timeout: 5000 };
// newConfig is now { host: ..., port: ..., timeout: 5000 }
```

Updated Application (2025): The End of the Date Object

For decades, the single most common source of bugs, frustration, and third-party libraries in JavaScript has been the Date object. It's mutable, its API is confusing, and it struggles with time zones.

As of 2025, this problem is officially solved. The Temporal API is the modern, robust replacement. It's built into the language (or available via a standard polyfill as it gains universal browser adoption) and provides a sane, predictable, and immutable way to handle date-time logic.

Let's say we're building a booking application. A user's booking is always for a specific calendar date, regardless of time zone.

Legacy Date (The Problem):
JavaScript

```
// A user in New York (GMT-4) books a hotel for November
20th
const bookingDate = new Date('2025-11-20T10:00:00-
04:00');
// A server in London (GMT+0) reads this...
console.log(bookingDate.toString());
// Output might be "Thu Nov 20 2025 14:00:00 GMT+0000"
// The date itself seems to have changed based on the
server's time zone.
```

Modern Temporal (The Solution):
JavaScript

```
// We want "November 20, 2025" in the ISO 8601 calendar,
period.
const plainDate = Temporal.PlainDate.from('2025-11-20');
console.log(plainDate.toString()); // "2025-11-20"

// Need the current date?
const today = Temporal.Now.plainDateISO();
```

```
console.log(today.toString()); // e.g., "2025-11-16"

// Need to add 30 days for a subscription?
const nextPaymentDate = today.add({ days: 30 });
console.log(nextPaymentDate.toString()); // e.g., "2025-12-16"
```

The logic is explicit, immutable (.add() returns a new object), and free of time zone "surprises." This is a monumental leap forward.

Real-Time Case Study: "The Good Parts" Revisited (2025)

In 2008, Douglas Crockford's JavaScript: The Good Parts was a revolutionary thesis. It argued that JavaScript was a brilliant language buried inside a bad one. He advised developers to avoid features like == (coercion), with, and global var.

Fast-forward to 2025, and this thesis is no longer just "advice"—it is the institutionalized, default-enforced standard of our entire ecosystem. Modern tools have codified his "good parts" into the workflow.

ESLint: A linter will scream at you (with red underlines) if you use == instead of ===. The "no-eq-null" rule is standard. It will warn you against var.

"Strict Mode": By writing 'use strict'; or just using ES6 Modules (which are strict by default), you opt into a "fixed" version of the language that throws errors instead of failing silently.

TypeScript: TypeScript, which is arguably the standard for large-scale applications, makes types explicit. Coercion-based errors are often caught at compile-time, before the code even runs.

Crockford's advice wasn't just adopted; it was automated. A junior developer today, using a standard setup (like Create React App or a Vite template), is protected from these legacy pitfalls by default.

Job Market Skills: Code Readability & Maintainability

This subtopic delivers the skill of Code Readability. A developer who understands these principles doesn't just write code that works. They write clean, modern, and predictable code. When a senior developer or hiring manager reviews your code, they see const, ===, and Temporal. They see a professional who avoids legacy pitfalls, embraces safer APIs, and writes code that is a pleasure to maintain, not a nightmare to debug.

2.2. Functions, Scope, and this: The Execution Context

If types are the "nouns" of JavaScript, the execution context—functions, scope, and the this keyword—is the "verb." This is the machinery that runs the code. Mastering it is the difference between a developer who guesses and a developer who knows.

The Foundations: Functions, Scope, and this

First, we must understand how JavaScript thinks about execution. Every time a function is called, a new execution context is created. This context has two key parts: its scope (what variables it can "see") and its this binding (what object it is called by).

JavaScript's "scope chain" is "lexical." This is a fancy term for a simple, beautiful rule: a function's scope is defined by where it is written in the code, not by where it is called.
JavaScript

```
const name = "Global";

function outer() {
  const name = "Outer";

  function inner() {
    // This 'name' is not defined inside 'inner',
    // so JS looks "up" to the 'outer' function.
    console.log(name);
  }

  inner();
}

outer(); // Prints "Outer"
```

The inner function will always have access to the name variable from outer, no matter where inner is eventually passed or called. This "remembering" of its birth-scope is called a closure.

Closures are the mechanism behind modern privacy and state. The module pattern? It's a closure. React's useState hook? It's a closure. A function "remembers" its state variable from a previous render.

The this keyword, however, is the opposite. Its value is not determined by where it's written, but by how the function is called. This creates five distinct rules that must be memorized:

Global: this is the global object (window in a browser).

Method: this is the object to the left of the dot (e.g., in user.greet(), this is user).

call/apply/bind: this is the object explicitly passed in.

Constructor: this is the new, empty object created by the new keyword.

Arrow Function: The game-changer. An arrow function (=>) has no this binding of its own. It lexically inherits this from its parent scope, just like any other variable.

Updated Application (2025): this in the Component Era

In 2025, the arrow function (Rule 5) is not just a convenience; it's the default, standard-practice solution for this binding, especially in component-based frameworks like React.

Before arrow functions, this in a React class was a constant source of pain.

Legacy Class (The Problem):
JavaScript

```
class LegacyCounter extends React.Component {
 constructor(props) {
  super(props);
  this.state = { count: 0 };
  // We had to manually "bind" this, or it would be
  // undefined when called by the button's click event.
  this.handleClick = this.handleClick.bind(this);
 }

 handleClick() {
  this.setState({ count: this.state.count + 1 });
 }

 render() {
```

```
    return <button
onClick={this.handleClick}>Click</button>;
  }
}
```

Modern Class/Callback (The Solution):
JavaScript

```
class ModernCounter extends React.Component {
  state = { count: 0 };

  // Use a class field with an arrow function.
  // This 'handleClick' lexically binds 'this' to
  // the class instance. No constructor 'bind' needed.
  handleClick = () => {
    this.setState({ count: this.state.count + 1 });
  }

  render() {
    return <button
onClick={this.handleClick}>Click</button>;
  }
}
```

This pattern is ubiquitous. Arrow functions provide a predictable, lexical this that just works, which is why they are the standard for event callbacks, .map functions, and anything inside a class method.

Real-Time Case Study: Debugging Legacy Code (e.g., jQuery/Backbone)

You're a new hire, and you're dropped into a 10-year-old application. It uses jQuery. You see this code:
JavaScript

```
$('.user-profile').each(function() {
```

```
  const userId = $(this).data('id'); // 'this' is the DOM
element

  // Now we make an AJAX call
  $.ajax({
    url: '/api/users/' + userId,
    success: function(data) {
      // BUG: 'this' is now something else!
      // It's not the DOM element anymore.
      // The 'success' callback sets its own 'this'.
      $(this).html(data.name); // This will fail or do weird
things.
    }
  });
});
```

This is a classic this binding error. The success callback is a new function call, and its this is set by the jQuery $.ajax internals, not by the outer function.

The old fix was a "closure variable," var self = this;. The modern, 2025-trained developer immediately spots this and refactors:

The Fix:
JavaScript

```
$('.user-profile').each(function() {
  const $element = $(this); // Store 'this' in a clear variable
  const userId = $element.data('id');

  $.ajax({
    url: '/api/users/' + userId,
    // Use an ARROW FUNCTION!
    success: (data) => {
      // 'this' is lexically inherited. Since arrow
      // functions don't have their own 'this', it
```

```
    // "sees" the 'this' from the outer '.each' function.
    $(this).html(data.name);
    // Or, even better:
    // $element.html(data.name);
  }
 });
});
```

Job Market Skills: Advanced Debugging

This knowledge provides the invaluable skill of Advanced Debugging. When you can trace and predict the value of this in any context, you can solve a class of bugs that leaves other developers mystified. This is a common and complex technical interview challenge. Being able to calmly explain the five this binding rules and identify the fix (almost always an arrow function) demonstrates a level of seniority and deep understanding that companies are desperate to hire.

2.3. Object-Oriented JavaScript: Prototypes and ES6+ Classes

JavaScript has always been an object-oriented language, but its approach has historically confused developers coming from class-based languages like Java or C++. The 2025-ready developer must understand both of JavaScript's OOP systems: the "native" prototypal inheritance and the "modern" class syntax that sits on top of it.

The Foundations: Prototypes and the class Sugar

At its core, JavaScript's object model is simple: objects can be linked to other objects. This "link" is the prototype chain. When you try to access a property on an object, if it's not found, JavaScript "walks up" the prototype chain to its parent, and so on, until it finds the property or hits null.

Before 2015, we created this chain manually using "constructor functions" and manipulating prototype. It was powerful but syntactically awkward.

The ES6 class syntax, introduced in 2015, changed everything. It provided a clean, familiar syntax that developers from other backgrounds could immediately recognize.

JavaScript

```
class Vehicle {
  // The constructor function
  constructor(make, model) {
    this.make = make;
    this.model = model;
  }

  // A method on the prototype
  honk() {
    console.log("Beep beep!");
  }

  // A static method (on the class itself)
  static getSlogan() {
    return "We make vehicles!";
  }
}

class Car extends Vehicle {
  // Use 'super' to call the parent's constructor
  constructor(make, model, doors) {
    super(make, model);
    this.doors = doors;
  }
```

```
  // Override the parent's method
  honk() {
    console.log("Honk honk!");
  }
}

const myCar = new Car("Toyota", "Camry", 4);
myCar.honk(); // "Honk honk!"
```

It is vital to understand that class is "syntactic sugar." Under the hood, this is still creating a Vehicle constructor function and attaching honk to Vehicle.prototype. But this sugar is what we use 99% of the time because it's clean and clear.

The final piece of this model is "private" fields. By using the # prefix, we can create fields that are truly private to the class, un-discoverable from the outside.
JavaScript

```
class ApiService {
  #apiKey; // Truly private field

  constructor(key) {
    this.#apiKey = key;
  }

  fetchData(endpoint) {
    // We can use #apiKey inside the class
    return
fetch(`https://api.example.com/${endpoint}?key=${this.#
apiKey}`);
  }
}

const service = new ApiService("my-secret-key");
```

```
console.log(service.#apiKey); // SyntaxError! Cannot
access private field.
```

Updated Application (2025): OOP in Service Classes

This class-based, object-oriented model is the standard for structuring a modern client-side application. While components (like in React or Vue) handle the view, we use OOP to handle the logic. This is a core tenet of software engineering: encapsulation and separation of concerns.

Instead of writing fetch calls directly inside our UI components, we build extensible, object-oriented service classes, just like the ApiService example.

JavaScript

```
// AuthService.js
// This class encapsulates ALL authentication logic.
class AuthService {
 #token = null;

 login(username, password) {
  // ... logic to fetch token
  this.#token = "...fetched-token...";
  localStorage.setItem("authToken", this.#token);
 }

 logout() {
  this.#token = null;
  localStorage.removeItem("authToken");
 }

 // A "getter"
 get isAuthenticated() {
  return this.#token !== null;
 }
```

```
  // A private helper
  #refreshToken() {
    // ...
  }
}

// Export a single instance (Singleton pattern)
export const authService = new AuthService();
```

Now, any component in our app can simply import { authService } and call authService.login() or check authService.isAuthenticated. The component doesn't need to know how the token is stored or fetched. That logic is perfectly encapsulated, testable, and maintainable.

Real-Time Case Study: React's Component Model

This brings us to a "real-time" case study: the component frameworks themselves. React, Vue, and Angular are all direct applications of OOP principles, whether they use the class keyword or not.

A React component (whether it's a class or a modern function) is a perfect example of an object.

Encapsulation: It bundles its own state (its data) and its behavior (its methods, like handleClick) into one self-contained unit.

Abstraction: It hides its internal complexity (e.g., a complex useEffect hook or componentDidMount logic) behind a simple interface (the component tag: <MyComponent />).

Composition: We build complex UIs by nesting components inside each other, just as we build complex objects from smaller ones.

A functional component with hooks is just a more "functional" way of achieving the same OOP goals. useState encapsulates state. useEffect encapsulates side-effects and lifecycle. The core principles of software design—encapsulation and abstraction—are the same.

Job Market Skills: Software Design

This knowledge provides the skill of Software Design. When you move beyond simple scripting and start thinking in terms of classes, services, and encapsulation, you are no longer just a "coder"—you are a "software engineer." You can structure and organize a complex application. You know how to separate concerns, write testable code, and build systems that can scale. This is the skill that gets you from a junior to a senior-level position.

2.4. New in ECMAScript 2025: The 16th Edition

A 2025 curriculum must be built on the 2025 standard. This subtopic is about the "newly formed content"—the features finalized in the 16th Edition of ECMA-262. Adopting these new, native language features allows us to write smaller, faster, and more maintainable code by replacing what used to require heavy external libraries.

The Foundations: What's New in ES2025

The ECMAScript 2025 specification, finalized in June 2025, brings several long-awaited, highly ergonomic features to the language.

New Set Methods: Set has always been great for unique collections, but performing operations between sets was clumsy. ES2025 adds a full suite of mathematical set methods:

Set.prototype.intersection(other): Returns a new set with elements in both sets.

Set.prototype.union(other): Returns a new set with elements from either set.

Set.prototype.difference(other): Returns a new set with elements only in the first set.

Set.prototype.symmetricDifference(other): Returns a new set with elements in one but not both sets.

Set.prototype.isSubsetOf(other), isSupersetOf(other), isDisjointFrom(other)

Iterator Helpers: Iterators (and generators) are powerful for lazy-loading data, but using them required manual for...of loops. Now, iterators get their own chainable methods, just like arrays:

.map(fn)

.filter(fn)

.take(n) (Get the first n items)

.drop(n) (Skip the first n items)

.toArray() (To finally collect the results)

RegExp.escape(): This is the 15-year-overdue native method to safely escape user input for use in a regular expression. It ensures a user's string is treated as a literal string, not as regex commands.

Promise.try(): This new static method starts a Promise chain with synchronous code that might throw an error. It unifies try...catch and .catch() blocks, allowing you to start a promise chain and catch any error (sync or async) with a single .catch().

Updated Application (2025): Security and Data Analysis

These new features have immediate, practical applications.

Security: Let's fix a common injection-style vulnerability. We have a search bar and want to highlight the user's search term.

The Vulnerability (Legacy Code):
JavaScript

```
function highlight(userInput, text) {
  // If userInput is ".*", this will match EVERYTHING.
  // If userInput is "(", this will throw a SyntaxError.
  const regex = new RegExp(userInput, 'gi');
  return text.replace(regex, `<mark>${userInput}</mark>`);
}
```

The Fix (ES2025):
JavaScript

```
function highlight(userInput, text) {
  // RegExp.escape() turns '.*' into '\.\*'
  // It turns '(' into '\('
  const escapedInput = RegExp.escape(userInput);
  const regex = new RegExp(escapedInput, 'gi');
  return text.replace(regex, `<mark>${userInput}</mark>`);
```

```
}
```

We just fixed a security and stability bug by replacing it with a single, standard language feature.

Data Analysis: Now, let's find common elements between two large data sets.

The Old Way (Lodash or manual loops):
JavaScript

```javascript
// We had to import a utility library
import _ from 'lodash';
const premiumUsers = new Set([1, 5, 20]);
const activeUsers = new Set([1, 2, 5, 10]);
const premiumAndActive = _.intersection(
  [...premiumUsers], [...activeUsers]
);
```

The New Way (ES2025 Native):
JavaScript

```javascript
const premiumUsers = new Set([1, 5, 20]);
const activeUsers = new Set([1, 2, 5, 10]);

// No library, no array conversion. It's native.
const premiumAndActive =
premiumUsers.intersection(activeUsers);
// premiumAndActive is a new Set: {1, 5}
```

Our code is smaller (no lodash bundle), faster (native engine implementation), and more readable.

Real-Time Case Study: The TC39 Proposal Pipeline

How did a feature like RegExp.escape "evolve"? It's not magic; it's a human-driven process. This case study is the TC39 (Technical Committee 39) "Proposal Pipeline."

Features evolve through five stages:

Stage 0 (Strawperson): An idea. "Hey, wouldn't RegExp.escape be nice?"

Stage 1 (Proposal): A formal proposal is written by a "champion" (a TC39 member) identifying the problem and a solution.

Stage 2 (Draft): The committee has accepted the feature. The exact "shape" (the API) is being actively designed and debated.

Stage 3 (Candidate): The design is final. This is the "go-ahead" for browser vendors (like Google's V8 or Apple's JavaScriptCore) to start implementing it. We can start using it with polyfills.

Stage 4 (Finished): The feature is implemented and tested in at least two major browsers. It is officially "done" and will be included in the next ECMAScript specification.

RegExp.escape, Set Methods, and Iterator Helpers all completed this journey to Stage 4 and were formally adopted into the ES2025 standard. This teaches us how to "see the future" by tracking what's currently in Stage 3.

Job Market Skills: Writing Future-Proof Code

This delivers the skill of Writing Future-Proof Code. A developer who understands the TC39 pipeline and embraces new, standardized features is highly valuable.

Advanced Asynchronous Programming and Modern Patterns

3.1. Asynchronous JavaScript: Callbacks, Promises, and async/await

At its very core, JavaScript is single-threaded. This is a fundamental concept that every developer must internalize. It means JavaScript can only do one thing at one single moment in time. This seems like a massive limitation. How can you possibly build a responsive web browser, let alone a high-performance server, if it can only process one command at a time? If it's busy downloading a large image (an I/O or "Input/Output" operation), does the entire user interface just freeze?

In the early days, the answer was often "yes." But the solution that made JavaScript viable is its asynchronous, non-blocking event loop. Instead of waiting for a task (like a network request or a file read) to finish, JavaScript says: "Okay, go do that task. I'm not going to wait for you. Just let me know when you're done, and I'll deal with the result. In the meantime, I'm moving on to the next thing."

This "let me know when you're done" mechanism is the entire basis of asynchronous programming.

The Problem: "Callback Hell"

The first way we handled this was with callbacks. A callback is just a function you pass as an argument to another function, which then gets "called back" when the task is complete.

It seems simple enough.

JavaScript

```
// A simple callback
fs.readFile('/my-file.txt', (err, data) => {
 if (err) {
  console.error('Oh no!', err);
  return;
 }
 console.log('File data:', data);
});
```

This is fine for one operation. But what if you need to perform sequential operations? What if you need to read a file, then use its contents to make an API call, then use that result to write to another file?

You get this:
JavaScript

```
// The "Pyramid of Doom"
fs.readFile('/file1.txt', (err1, data1) => {
 if (err1) {
  handleError(err1);
 } else {
  // Got file 1, now make API call
  api.fetchData(data1, (err2, data2) => {
   if (err2) {
    handleError(err2);
   } else {
    // Got API data, now write to file 2
    fs.writeFile('/file2.txt', data2, (err3) => {
     if (err3) {
      handleError(err3);
     } else {
      console.log('All done!');
      // What if we need a *fourth* step?
      // The pyramid just keeps growing...
```

```
        }
      });
    }
  });
}
});
```

This is what we call "Callback Hell," or the "Pyramid of Doom." From my own experience in maintaining legacy code, this is more than just ugly. It's a genuine liability. Error handling is a nightmare—each step needs its own if (err) check. Debugging is a treasure hunt. Trying to refactor or add a new step is like playing Jenga with a live grenade. This code is brittle, hard to read, and impossible to maintain.

The Solution: Promise Objects

The community needed a better way. In ES2015, Promises were standardized. A Promise is an object that represents the eventual completion (or failure) of an asynchronous operation.

Think of it as a receipt. When you order a coffee, you don't stand at the counter staring at the barista. They give you a receipt (a Promise) and you go sit down. That receipt promises you'll either get your coffee (it's fulfilled) or be told they're out of beans (it's rejected).

A Promise has three states:

pending: The initial state. The coffee order is in.

fulfilled: The operation completed successfully. You got your coffee.

rejected: The operation failed. They're out of beans.

The real power of Promises is that they can be chained. They have methods like .then() (which runs on fulfillment) and .catch() (which runs on rejection).

Let's refactor that pyramid:

JavaScript

```
// We'll "promisify" the fs function first
import { promises as fs } from 'fs';

fs.readFile('/file1.txt')
  .then(data1 => {
    // data1 is the *result* of the first promise
    return api.fetchData(data1); // Return a *new* promise
  })
  .then(data2 => {
    // data2 is the *result* of the second promise
    return fs.writeFile('/file2.txt', data2); // Return a *new*
promise
  })
  .then(() => {
    // This .then() runs after the writeFile is done
    console.log('All done!');
  })
  .catch(err => {
    // ONE catch block for *any* error in the chain!
    handleError(err);
  });
```

The pyramid is gone. It's a flat, readable, top-to-bottom chain. And best of all, a single .catch() at the end will handle any failure from readFile, fetchData, or writeFile. This was a revolutionary leap in maintainability.

The Syntactic Sugar: async/await

Promises are fantastic, but the chaining with .then() can still feel a bit unnatural. In ES2017, JavaScript gave us async/await.

This is the most important part to understand: async/await is just "syntactic sugar" on top of Promises. It does not replace Promises; it just gives us a cleaner way to write them.

The async keyword: You put this before a function declaration (async function myFunc() {}). It tells JavaScript, "This function will always return a Promise."

The await keyword: You can only use this inside an async function. You put it in front of any function that returns a Promise (like fetch() or our fs.readFile() promise). It tells JavaScript, "Pause the execution of this function only until this Promise settles (is fulfilled or rejected)."

Let's do that refactor one more time. This is the 2025 standard.
JavaScript

```
// Updated Application (2025 Refactor)
import { promises as fs } from 'fs';

async function performOperations() {
  try {
    // It *looks* synchronous
    const data1 = await fs.readFile('/file1.txt');

    // This line won't run until readFile is fulfilled
    const data2 = await api.fetchData(data1);

    // This line won't run until fetchData is fulfilled
```

```
    await fs.writeFile('/file2.txt', data2);

    console.log('All done!');
  } catch (err) {
    // We can use a standard, familiar try/catch block!
    handleError(err);
  }
}

performOperations();
```

Look at that. The code is clean. It's readable from top to bottom, just like synchronous code. Error handling uses the try/catch block every programmer already understands. This clarity is why async/await is the non-negotiable standard.

A real-world investigation proves this point. Look at Patreon's 2024 migration to Next.js. They detailed a massive "no-downtime overhaul" of their entire architecture. A core part of this is how Next.js handles data fetching using functions like getServerSideProps. That function's signature is literally export async function getServerSideProps(context). It demands asynchronous, Promise-based code. Patreon's critical server-side data (user info, campaign details) is all fetched using this async/await standard before a page can even be rendered.

This brings us to the Job Market Skill: Asynchronous Flow Control. This is, without a doubt, the most-tested JavaScript concept in technical interviews. They'll give you a callback-based problem and ask you to refactor it. They're not just testing if you know the syntax. They're testing if you understand why. Can you write code that is non-blocking, robust, and clean? Mastery of async/await demonstrates all three.

3.2. Advanced Promise Patterns and ES2024/2025 Enhancements

Once you've mastered async/await for sequential tasks, the next question is: "What about parallel tasks?"

Imagine you're loading a user's dashboard. You need to fetch their profile info, their recent notifications, and their list of friends.

A junior developer might write:
JavaScript

```javascript
// BAD: This is a "request waterfall"
const profile = await fetch('/api/profile');
const notifications = await fetch('/api/notifications'); // Waits for profile
const friends = await fetch('/api/friends'); // Waits for notifications
```

This is slow. These three requests are not dependent on each other. You're waiting for each one to finish before starting the next, creating a "waterfall" of network requests.

The correct approach is to fire them all off at the same time and wait for them all to come back. This is where Promise combinators come in.

The Core Combinators: all, allSettled, race

Promise.all(): This is the "all or nothing" combinator. It takes an array of Promises and returns a single new Promise. This new Promise only fulfills if every single Promise in the array fulfills. If even one of them rejects, the entire Promise.all immediately rejects.

Use Case: Critical data. For our dashboard, if we must have the profile, notifications, and friends list to render the page at all, Promise.all is perfect.

JavaScript

```
try {
  const [profileRes, notificationsRes, friendsRes] = await
Promise.all([
    fetch('/api/profile'),
    fetch('/api/notifications'),
    fetch('/api/friends')
  ]);
  // All three are back! Now we can process them.
  const profile = await profileRes.json();
  const notifications = await notificationsRes.json();
  // ...
} catch (err) {
  // If *any* of them failed, we end up here.
  showDashboardErrorPage();
}
```

Promise.allSettled(): This is the "wait for all, regardless of failure" combinator. This is, in my experience, often more useful for UI development. What if the "friends list" widget isn't critical? What if it fails, but we still want to show the profile and notifications?

Promise.allSettled waits for every Promise to "settle" (either fulfill or reject). It never rejects. It always fulfills with an array of status objects that tell you how each individual promise did.

Use Case (Dashboard Loading): The 2025 application. Let's build a resilient dashboard.

JavaScript

```
const results = await Promise.allSettled([
  fetch('/api/profile'), // Critical
  fetch('/api/widget-a'), // Non-critical
  fetch('/api/widget-b')  // Non-critical
]);

// results is an array like:
// [
//   { status: 'fulfilled', value: Response_Profile },
//   { status: 'fulfilled', value: Response_WidgetA },
//   { status: 'rejected',  reason: Error_WidgetB }
// ]

if (results[0].status === 'fulfilled') {
  renderProfile(await results[0].value.json());
} else {
  showFatalError(); // Profile was critical, it failed
}

if (results[1].status === 'fulfilled') {
  renderWidgetA(await results[1].value.json());
} else {
  showErrorInWidgetA(results[1].reason); // Show a small
error icon
}

// ...and so on for Widget B.
```

This allows the UI to render successfully even if one or two non-critical API calls fail. This is robust, modern front-end design.

Promise.race(): This is the "first one to finish wins." It takes an array of Promises and settles as soon as one of them settles.

Use Case: Implementing a timeout. This is a classic pattern. You "race" your data-fetching Promise against a setTimeout Promise.

JavaScript

```
const timeout = new Promise((_, reject) =>
  setTimeout(() => reject(new Error('Request timed out')),
5000)
);

try {
  const response = await Promise.race([
    fetch('/api/slow-resource'),
    timeout
  ]);
  // If we get here, fetch() won *before* the 5-second
timeout
  const data = await response.json();
} catch (err) {
  // We get here if *either* fetch() rejected *or* the
timeout won
  console.error(err.message); // Will be 'Request timed
out' if timeout won
}
```

Newest Enhancements (ES2024 / ES2025)

The language is still evolving.

Promise.withResolvers() (ES2024): This is a new utility that solves a long-standing "messy code" problem. Sometimes, you need to create a Promise but resolve or reject it from outside the constructor. A classic case is waiting for a WebSocket message or a DOM event. Before, you had to declare let resolvePromise in a higher scope and assign it inside the constructor. It was clunky. Promise.withResolvers() simplifies this vastly.

```
JavaScript

// Application: Wait for a WebSocket message
const { promise, resolve, reject } =
Promise.withResolvers();

// We can pass `resolve` to *any* other part of our code
webSocket.onmessage = (event) => {
  resolve(event.data); // Resolve the promise when the
message arrives
};

webSocket.onerror = (err) => {
  reject(err); // Reject it on an error
};

// Now, in our async function, we can just...
console.log('Waiting for socket message...');
const message = await promise; // This will pause until
onmessage calls resolve()
console.log('Got message:', message);
```

Promise.try() (Stage 3, expected ES2025): This utility is for advanced error handling. What if your code before the async operation throws an error? A .catch() on a Promise chain won't catch synchronous errors that happen during its creation. Promise.try() creates a new Promise that immediately executes a function. If that function (even if synchronous) throws an error, it returns a Promise that rejects with that error. It guarantees that all errors, sync or async, are funneled into the Promise rejection chain.

This brings us to the Real-Time Case Study: Shopify's Admin Performance (2025). My research into their "Remixing Shopify's Admin" project shows a 30% speed increase. This doesn't happen by accident. It's achieved through sophisticated parallel data fetching. When you load an "Order" page, they don't do a waterfall. They use patterns identical to Promise.all to fetch the Order details, Customer details, Product details, and Shipping details simultaneously on the server. This heavy optimization is a real-world example of the Job Market Skill: Advanced API Orchestration. This skill means you can design complex, parallel, and dependent API calls that maximize performance and resilience.

3.3. Data Handling: Iterators, Generators, and Streams

We've mastered when data arrives (async). Now let's master how data arrives, especially when it's too big to handle all at once.

What if you have to process a 5-gigabyte log file? Or an API that returns a list of 10 million users? You cannot load that into memory. A Node.js server will crash. A browser will freeze. The traditional model of const data = await response.json() breaks down completely at scale.

This is where we move from "data in a variable" to "data as a sequence."

The Iterator Protocol and Generators

First, we need a common language for "sequences." This is the Iterator Protocol. It's a simple contract: an object is an "iterator" if it has a .next() method that returns an object with two properties: { value, done }.

value: The current item in the sequence.

done: A boolean. false if there are more items, true if the sequence is finished.

JavaScript's for...of loop understands this protocol perfectly.

But how do you create an iterator easily? With Generator Functions (function*). A generator is a "pausable function." You define it with a function* syntax. When you call it, it doesn't run. It returns an iterator.

The magic keyword is yield. When the .next() method is called on its iterator, the generator function runs until it hits a yield, pauses its execution, and "yields" that value.

Application (Lazy Loading): Let's use a generator to lazily fetch paginated data. The consumer of this function won't even know it's making network requests.

JavaScript

```
// A "pausable" function
async function* getPaginatedUsers() {
  let page = 1;
  let hasMore = true;

  while (hasMore) {
    console.log(`Fetching page ${page}...`);
    const response = await
fetch(`/api/users?page=${page}`);
    const data = await response.json();

    if (data.users.length === 0) {
      hasMore = false;
    } else {
      // 'yield' will *pause* the function here
      // and send this value to the consumer
      yield data.users;
      page++;
    }
```

```
  }
  console.log('No more users.');
}

// The Consumer:
(async () => {
  // We create the iterator. Nothing has run yet.
  const userIterator = getPaginatedUsers();

  // We use 'for await...of' for an *async* iterator
  for await (const userBatch of userIterator) {
    // The loop body runs. 'userBatch' is the array from
`yield data.users`
    console.log(`Got a batch of ${userBatch.length}
users`);
    // The loop pauses here, waiting for the *next* yield
  }
})();

// Output:
// Fetching page 1...
// Got a batch of 50 users
// Fetching page 2...
// Got a batch of 50 users
// Fetching page 3...
// No more users.
```

We are processing all users without ever holding more than one "page" in memory. This is incredibly powerful and memory-efficient.

Asynchronous Iterators and Streams

The for await...of syntax we just used is for asynchronous iterators. It's an iterator where the .next() method itself returns a Promise (which resolves to the { value, done } object).

This brings us to the final concept: Streams. Streams are the built-in implementation of this concept in Node.js (and increasingly, in the browser with the Streams API). A stream is an iterator for data that flows in "chunks."

Think of it as a river. You don't "get" the river. You dip your bucket in and get a "chunk" of water. Streams in Node.js are built on this. fs.createReadStream doesn't read the file; it gives you a "readable stream" (an async iterator) that emits chunks of data from that file as they are read from the disk.

Application (Big Data): The 2025 standard for processing a large file. We will pipe the data through transformers without ever holding it all.

JavaScript

```
import { createReadStream } from 'fs';
import { createGzip } from 'zlib'; // To compress it
import { createWriteStream } from 'fs';

// 1. Create a stream *from* our 5GB log file
const sourceStream = createReadStream('huge.log');

// 2. Create a transform stream to compress the data
const gzipStream = createGzip();

// 3. Create a stream *to* our new destination file
const destinationStream =
createWriteStream('huge.log.gz');

// 4. Connect them. This is the 'pipe'

sourceStream.pipe(gzipStream).pipe(destinationStream);

// We can listen for events
```

```
  destinationStream.on('finish', () => {
    console.log('Successfully compressed 5GB file!');
  });
```

At no point during this operation was the 5GB file in memory. We used maybe a few megabytes of "buffer" memory as the chunks flowed through the pipeline. This is the only way to handle data at this scale.

The Real-Time Case Study: Netflix's Data-Intensive Platform is a perfect example. My analysis of their tech stack shows that Node.js is a critical part of their architecture. Why? Because Node.js is purpose-built for this kind of high-I/O, stream-based processing. They handle massive data streams for real-time analytics (who is watching what, right now) and for content delivery itself. This concept of streaming is the core Job Market Skill: Large-Scale Data Handling. This skill demonstrates you can design memory-efficient solutions. It's the key differentiator for back-end and data-intensive roles, proving you can write code that doesn't just work, but scales.

3.4. Data Structures and Immutability (ES2025+ Update)

Finally, let's talk about the data itself. We've covered when and how it arrives. Now let's talk about how to manage it safely once we have it. This leads to one of the most important (and often misunderstood) principles in modern software: immutability.

Immutability means "unchangeable." The principle is simple: once a piece of data (an object or array) is created, you never change it. If you need a modified version, you create a new one with the changes.

The "Why": React State Management

Why on earth would we do this? It sounds inefficient. The answer lies in change detection.

The Real-Time Case Study: React State Management is the defining example. Let's say you have a "shopping cart" in React state: const [cart, setCart] = useState(['apples', 'oranges']);

A junior developer might try to add an item like this:
JavaScript

```
// THIS IS WRONG.
function addItem() {
  cart.push('grapes'); // This is a "mutation"
  setCart(cart); // We give React the *same* array back
}
```

React will re-render, and... nothing will change on the screen. Why?

React's performance optimization relies on a simple check: "Did the state change?" To do this, it checks if (oldState === newState). In JavaScript, arrays and objects are compared by reference (their address in memory). When you cart.push('grapes'), you mutated the original array. It's still the same array in memory. So, oldState === newState is true, and React thinks nothing changed, so it bails on the re-render.

This is the correct, immutable way:
JavaScript

```
// THIS IS RIGHT.
function addItem() {
  // We create a *brand new array*
```

```
  const newCart = [...cart, 'grapes'];
  setCart(newCart); // We give React a *new reference*
}
```

Now, oldState === newState is false. React sees a new array, knows the state has changed, and correctly re-renders the UI. This is the core of Predictable State Management. By treating your state as immutable, you eliminate an entire class of "heisenbugs" where data changes mysteriously.

Modern Tools for Immutability

This pattern used to be a little clunky. How do you "immutably" sort an array? You'd have to make a copy first: const newSortedArr = [...oldArr].sort().

JavaScript is now building these patterns directly into the language.

Immutable Array Methods (ES2023-2024): We now have immutable counterparts for mutating methods:

array.sort() (mutates) -> array.toSorted() (returns a new sorted array)

array.splice() (mutates) -> array.toSpliced() (returns a new array with the splice applied)

array.reverse() (mutates) -> array.toReversed() (returns a new reversed array)

array.with(index, value) (returns a new array with the value at index changed)

This makes immutable updates much more ergonomic.

Object.groupBy() and Map.groupBy() (ES2024): This is a massive quality-of-life improvement. A common task is to take a flat array of data and group it. Before, this was a complex, error-prone reduce function. Now, it's one line.

Application (Data Transformation): Let's group an array of user objects by their country.

JavaScript

```
const users = [
  { name: 'Alice', country: 'USA' },
  { name: 'Bob', country: 'UK' },
  { name: 'Charlie', country: 'USA' }
];

// The old, hard-to-read way:
const oldGrouped = users.reduce((acc, user) => {
  (acc[user.country] = acc[user.country] ||
[]).push(user);
  return acc;
}, {});

// The new, clean, 2025 way:
const newGrouped = Object.groupBy(users, user =>
user.country);

// The result is clean and instant:
// {
//   "USA": [ { name: 'Alice', ... }, { name: 'Charlie', ... } ],
//   "UK": [ { name: 'Bob', ... } ]
// }
```

This is less code, but more importantly, it's declarative. It says what to do, not how to do it, which is easier to read and impossible to get wrong.

The Future: Record & Tuple (ES2025+)

The "final frontier" for immutability in JavaScript is the Record & Tuple proposal (currently at Stage 2, but a high-priority feature). These will be truly immutable data structures, built right into the language.

Records: #{ key: 'value' } (using #{...})

Like an Object, but completely frozen. You cannot add, change, or delete properties.

Tuples: #[1, 2, 'three'] (using #[...])

Like an Array, but completely frozen. You cannot push, pop, or change values.

The most revolutionary part? They will be compared by value, not by reference. #[1, 2] === #[1, 2] will be true.

This will have a profound impact on performance and state management. React's if (oldState === newState) check will become trivial and deeply accurate, no longer just a shallow reference check.

This all ladders up to the final Job Market Skill: Predictable State Management. When an interviewer asks you about immutability, they're not asking for a dictionary definition. They are asking if you understand why modern frameworks (React, Vue, Angular, Svelte) are all built on this principle. It shows you can write clean, bug-free code that works with the framework, not against it, creating predictable, maintainable, and performant applications.

Part 2: Client-Side Software Engineering

The Browser Environment and Document Object Model (DOM)

4.1. The Browser as a Platform: APIs, Storage, and Security

The Misconception of the "Viewer"

For a long time, many beginners—and even some intermediate developers—viewed the web browser simply as a document viewer. You give it an HTML file, and it paints it on the screen. However, if you look at the curriculum of MIT 6.4500 or Stanford CS142, you quickly realize this is a dangerous oversimplification.

In 2025, the browser is not a viewer; it is a fully-fledged operating system. It has its own file system access, its own network layer, and a rigid security model. If you treat it like a PDF reader, you will build insecure software.

The Security Foundation: Same-Origin Policy (SOP)

The absolute bedrock of web security is the Same-Origin Policy (SOP). Imagine living in an apartment complex. You have a key to your apartment (your "origin"). The SOP is the rule that says your key cannot open your neighbor's door, nor can your neighbor's key open yours.

Technically, an "origin" is defined by three things: the Protocol (https), the Host (https://www.google.com/search?q=google.com), and the Port (443). If any one of these differs, the browser erects a wall. Without this, a malicious script on evil-site.com could simply read the emails open in your gmail.com tab.

Client-Side Storage: A Practical Guide to "Where to Put Data"

One of the most common debates in engineering teams is state management. "Where do we store the data?" In 2025, we have clear, distinct lanes for this, and mixing them up is a security vulnerability waiting to happen.

Local Storage: This is like a persistent locker. It stays there until you delete it. It is perfect for non-sensitive UI preferences.

Example: If a user toggles "Dark Mode" or minimizes a specific dashboard widget, save that boolean value here. If an attacker steals this via Cross-Site Scripting (XSS), the worst thing that happens is the user's theme changes.

Session Storage: This is temporary. It dies when the tab closes.

Example: This is great for multi-step form data (e.g., an airline checkout flow) where you want the data to vanish if the user rage-quits the page.

Cookies (The Security Critical Layer): This is where authentication lives.

The Stanford "Cookie Management" Approach

In Stanford's CS142 projects, students often face the harsh reality of session management. Here is the standard for 2025 that separates junior developers from seniors: Never store JSON Web Tokens (JWTs) or session IDs in LocalStorage.

If you store a session token in LocalStorage, any JavaScript running on your page (including that third-party analytics script you didn't audit) can read it. Instead, we use HttpOnly Cookies.

When a user logs in via the fetch API, the server should respond with a Set-Cookie header. You must configure this cookie with three specific flags:

HttpOnly: This makes the cookie invisible to JavaScript. document.cookie returns nothing. This neutralizes XSS attacks regarding auth theft.

Secure: The cookie is only sent over encrypted HTTPS connections.

SameSite: This helps prevent Cross-Site Request Forgery (CSRF) by telling the browser not to send the cookie if the request comes from an external site.

The Network Layer: The Fetch API

Gone are the days of the clunky XMLHttpRequest. The Fetch API is the modern standard, using "Promises" to handle the asynchronous nature of the web.

Real-World Scenario: When you load a user profile, the browser doesn't freeze. You fire a fetch request. While that request travels across the ocean to a data center, the browser continues rendering the rest of the page. When the data returns (as a JSON object), the Promise resolves, and you update the UI. This non-blocking behavior is what makes the web feel fluid.

4.2. DOM Manipulation: The "Vanilla" JavaScript Approach

Why We Start "Naked"

There is a reason top universities and bootcamps force you to write "Vanilla" (plain) JavaScript before touching React, Vue, or Angular. React is an abstraction. It is a layer of paint over the raw machinery of the Document Object Model (DOM). If you don't understand the machinery, you cannot fix it when the abstraction leaks.

The DOM Tree

The DOM is a tree structure. The "Root" is the document. Every tag—<div>, <p>, <span>—is a node (branch or leaf) on that tree.

Traversal and Selection To change something, you first have to find it. We use document.querySelector() for this. It uses the same syntax as CSS.

Example: document.querySelector('.submit-btn') finds the first element with the class submit-btn. This is the digital equivalent of pointing your finger at a specific item on a shelf.

Manipulation: The CRUD of the DOM Once you have the element, you perform operations. This is often taught through the classic "To-Do List" Project, a staple in curriculums like Berkeley CS198 and Stanford CS142.

Create: You use document.createElement('li') to conjure a new list item into existence in memory. It isn't visible yet; it's just a floating object.

Update: You add text: newItem.textContent = "Buy Milk".

Read/Append: You must attach it to the DOM tree to make it visible: list.appendChild(newItem).

Delete: You use newItem.remove() to detach it from the tree.

Event Propagation: Bubbling vs. Capturing

This is the concept that trips up 90% of new developers during interviews. When you click a button inside a div, inside a section, inside the body, you aren't just clicking the button. You are clicking all of them.

Bubbling: Imagine blowing a bubble underwater. It floats up to the surface. When an event happens, it starts at the target (the button) and "bubbles up" to the parents. This allows for a powerful pattern called Event Delegation.

Practical Application: Instead of adding 100 event listeners to 100 items in your To-Do list (which eats up memory), you add one listener to the parent <ul>. When a user clicks an item, the event bubbles up to the <ul>, and you check event.target to see which item was actually clicked. This is an optimization technique used in high-performance applications.

Real-Time Case Study: Wingify's VWO Editor (2024)

Wingify, the company behind VWO (a massive A/B testing platform), provided a fascinating case study in 2024 regarding this. They built a visual editor that allows marketing teams to change the text or color of a website without coding.

While the customers use a GUI, the underlying engine uses aggressive, raw DOM manipulation. They inject a script that must traverse the client's website DOM, identify elements despite dynamic class names, and force style changes. They found that frameworks like React were too heavy and opinionated for this specific task. They had to use pure, vanilla JavaScript to ensure their editor worked on any website, regardless of whether that site was built with WordPress, React, or raw HTML. This proves that "Framework Interoperability"—the ability to write code that works outside of a framework—is a critical, high-level job skill.

4.3. Modern Browser APIs: Building Richer Applications

Closing the Gap with Native Apps

For years, "Native" mobile apps (iOS/Android) were superior to web apps because they could work offline and had push notifications. In subtopic 4.3, we explore how the browser has closed this gap. The browser is now a "platform" capable of running near-native software.

WebSockets: True Real-Time Communication

Before WebSockets, if you wanted to check for new messages in a chat app, you had to use "Polling." This is like a child in the backseat asking, "Are we there yet?" every 3 seconds. It wastes battery and bandwidth.

WebSockets changed this. It opens a permanent, two-way tunnel between the client and the server.

The Analogy: It is like a telephone call. The line stays open. Neither party has to dial again; they just speak.

Application: In a 2025 chat application, when User A types a message, the server pushes it down the WebSocket pipe to User B instantly. No polling required.

Service Workers and PWAs (Progressive Web Apps)

A Service Worker is a script that your browser runs in the background, separate from a web page. It is the "air traffic controller" of the browser.

Offline Functionality: When you visit a site, the Service Worker can cache the HTML, CSS, and JS files. If you lose your internet connection (common on subways or airplanes), the Service Worker intercepts the network request. Seeing you are offline, it serves the cached files instead of a "No Internet" dinosaur error.

Background Sync: It can even queue up data. If you send a message while offline, the Service Worker holds it and fires it off the moment connectivity is restored.

Web Components: The End of Framework Lock-In?

This is the most significant trend of 2025. For the last decade, if you built a "Button" component in React, you couldn't use it in an Angular app. You had to rewrite it.

Web Components are a set of standards (Custom Elements, Shadow DOM, HTML Templates) that allow you to create your own HTML tags—like <my-super-button>—that work in any framework or no framework at all.

Shadow DOM: This is a crucial part of Web Components. It allows you to encapsulate CSS. Styles defined inside your <my-super-button> will not leak out and mess up the rest of the page, and global styles won't accidentally break your button.

Industry Shift: Large enterprises are now building their "Design Systems" using Web Components. This insulates them from the "Framework Wars." If they decide to switch from React to Svelte next year, their core library of buttons, inputs, and navbars remains exactly the same. This is the definition of "Platform-Native Development."

4.4. Layout and Rendering: HTML, CSS, and the Critical Path

The Mechanics of Pixels

Writing code is one thing; getting pixels onto the screen at 60 frames per second is another. This section deals with the Critical Rendering Path—the sequence of steps the browser takes to convert HTML, CSS, and JavaScript into actual sights on the screen.

The Critical Path Sequence

DOM Construction: The browser parses HTML into the DOM tree.

CSSOM Construction: It parses CSS into the CSS Object Model.

Render Tree: It combines the DOM and CSSOM. Crucially, invisible elements (like <head> or things with display: none) are excluded here.

Layout: The browser calculates the geometry. It figures out exactly how many pixels wide the "Submit" button is and where it sits relative to the edge of the screen.

Paint: The browser fills in the pixels (colors, shadows, text).

Performance Optimization: Layout Thrashing A major skill in "Front-End Performance Optimization" is avoiding Layout Thrashing.

The Scenario: Imagine you run a loop where you read an element's width, then double it, then read it again, then double it again.

The Problem: Every time you change the width, the browser has to re-calculate the geometry of the entire page (Reflow) before it can give you the new width. Doing this in a loop forces the browser into a frantic cycle of Read-Calculate-Read-Calculate. This kills performance and causes visual stuttering.

The Fix: Read all your values first (batch reading), then write all your changes (batch writing).

CSS Paradigms: The 2025 Debate

In 2025, the war between Semantic CSS and Utility-First CSS (Tailwind) is the defining conversation of frontend architecture.

Semantic CSS (The Stanford/Classic Way): You write HTML like <div class="profile-card"> and then have a separate CSS file defining .profile-card. This separates concerns. It keeps the HTML clean and readable. It is excellent for long-term maintainability and is strictly taught in accessibility-focused courses.

Utility-First (The Tailwind Way): You write HTML like <div class="flex p-4 bg-blue-500 rounded-lg">. You are applying styles directly in the HTML.

The Trade-off: Purists hate Tailwind because it clutters the HTML. Pragmatists love it because it speeds up development—you never have to leave your HTML file or invent names for wrapper divs.

The Industry Reality: Startups and rapid-prototyping environments are heavily leaning toward Tailwind. However, large-scale applications with strict accessibility and governance requirements often stick to Semantic CSS (or CSS Modules) to ensure the "Separation of Concerns" principle isn't violated.

Grid vs. Flexbox Finally, modern layout mastery requires knowing when to use Grid and when to use Flexbox.

Flexbox: One-dimensional. Use it for a row of buttons or a navigation bar.

CSS Grid: Two-dimensional. Use it for the overall page skeleton (Header, Sidebar, Main Content, Footer).

By mastering these layout engines and the performance cost of the rendering path, you ensure your application doesn't just work—it feels instant.

Front-End Frameworks: Architecture and Comparative Analysis

In the world of software engineering, tools change rapidly, but architecture endures. Before we write a single line of React code, we must understand the architectural vacuum that necessitated its creation. This chapter bridges the gap between basic JavaScript proficiency and professional systems design. We are moving from "how to code" to "how to design."

5.1 The Need for Frameworks: From DOM Manipulation to Declarative UIs

To understand the solution, you must first feel the pain of the problem. In the early days of the web, and even in modern "vanilla" JavaScript development, we interacted with the browser using Imperative Programming.

Imagine you are a taxi driver. An imperative passenger sits down and says: "Turn on the engine. Put the car in drive. Press the gas. Drive 500 meters. Turn right. Drive 200 meters. Stop."

This is how we used to talk to the browser. We manually selected elements and mutated them.

The Problem: The Fragility of State

In a complex application, your data is your "State." This includes the user's name, their unread messages, and the items in their shopping cart. The hardest part of UI engineering is not drawing pixels; it is keeping the UI in sync with that State.

When using manual DOM manipulation (like document.getElementById), you are responsible for manually updating every part of the screen whenever the data changes.

Consider the "Spaghetti" of Vanilla JS: If you delete an item from a list in plain JavaScript, you have to:

Find the specific DOM node in the HTML tree.

Remove the listener attached to it to prevent memory leaks.

Remove the node.

Recalculate the "Total Items" counter at the top of the page.

Update the "Empty State" message if the list is now empty.

If you forget step 4, your UI is lying to the user. As applications grow to thousands of interactions, this manual syncing becomes impossible to maintain. This is where "State Management" fails in imperative systems.

The Solution: Declarative UIs

Modern frameworks like React introduced a Declarative paradigm. Returning to our taxi analogy, a declarative passenger simply says: "Take me to the Airport."

They describe the destination (the desired state), not the turn-by-turn directions (the DOM updates). In React, you simply tell the framework: "Here is the data. The UI should look like this based on that data." When the data changes, the framework figures out how to update the screen.

2025 Updated Application: The Code Reality

Let's look at the difference. Here is the cognitive load required to update a list in both paradigms.

The Old Way (Imperative/Vanilla JS):
JavaScript

```
// We have to manually hunt down elements
const list = document.getElementById('user-list');
const newItem = document.createElement('li');
newItem.innerText = 'New User';

// We have to manually append
list.appendChild(newItem);

// We have to manually find and update the counter
const countDisplay =
document.getElementById('counter');
const currentCount = parseInt(countDisplay.innerText);
countDisplay.innerText = currentCount + 1;
```

The Modern Way (Declarative/React):
JavaScript

```
// We just update the data. The UI "reacts" automatically.
setUsers([...users, 'New User']);
```

In the second example, we never touched the DOM. We updated the State, and the UI reflected that change instantly.

Architectural Concept: The Virtual DOM

How does React do this without being slow? It uses a Virtual DOM (vDOM).

Imagine a blueprint of a house. If you want to move a couch, you don't tear down the house and rebuild it. You simply move the pencil mark on the blueprint. React creates a "virtual" copy of your UI in memory. When state changes, it compares the new virtual blueprint with the old one.

This process is called Reconciliation. It calculates the mathematical difference (diffing) and updates only the specific text node that changed in the real browser.
Update $\text{Complexity} \approx O(\text{nodes changed}) \text{vs.} O(\text{total nodes})$

Real-Time Case Study: React at Meta (The Chat Bug)

React was born out of frustration. In the early 2010s, Facebook had a famous "Zombie Notification" bug. You would see a red notification badge indicating a new message. You would click it, read the message, but the badge would stay red.

Why? Because their code was imperative. One team managed the chat box, another managed the notification bar. When a user read a message, the chat box updated, but the notification bar "missed" the memo. The state was out of sync.

Meta engineers realized they couldn't keep manually stitching these updates together. They built React to ensure that if the underlying data (State) says "0 unread messages," the UI automatically renders "0," regardless of which component is asking.

Job Market Insight: When interviewing for Senior roles, do not just say "React is cool." Explain that you choose frameworks because they reduce the cognitive load of state synchronization, allowing teams to scale without creating brittle code.

5.2 Component-Based Architecture: The Building Blocks of Modern UI

Once we accept that we need a framework, we must understand how to structure our application. The fundamental atom of modern web development is the Component.

The Philosophy of Encapsulation

In the past, we separated technologies. We had a folder for HTML (structure), a folder for CSS (style), and a folder for JS (logic).

Component architecture changes this. Instead of separating technologies, we separate concerns. A "Button" component contains its own HTML, its own CSS, and its own Click Logic all in one file. This is Encapsulation. It ensures that if you delete the Button component, you delete all its associated code, leaving no "dead CSS" behind.

Composition: The LEGO Model

We build complex applications by composing simple components together.

- An Atom might be a Label or an Input box.
- A Molecule combines them into a "Search Bar."

A Organism places the Search Bar into a "Header."

Data Flow: Props vs. State

Understanding the flow of data is the most critical skill in component design. We distinguish between two types of data:

Props (Properties): This is data passed into a component. It is immutable. Think of it like a biological trait passed from parent to child. A child component cannot change its own Props.

State: This is data managed within a component. It is mutable. This is the component's short-term memory.

The Principle of One-Way Data Flow: In a healthy architecture, data flows down like a waterfall. ParentPropsChildPropsGrandchild

Events (like clicks) flow up. If a child needs to change data, it doesn't touch the data directly. It calls a function passed down by the parent, asking the parent to change it. This ensures that the Parent remains the "Single Source of Truth."

Updated Application: Decomposing Spotify

Let's play the role of an architect. Look at a screenshot of the Spotify Desktop Player. How do we break this down?

The Container (Smart Component): The MusicPlayer wrapper. This holds the State: What song is playing? Is it paused?

The Presentational (Dumb Components):

PlayButton: It doesn't know what song is playing. It just knows it is a triangle shape. When clicked, it notifies the Container.

ProgressBar: It receives a number (e.g., "50%") via Props from the Container. It creates the visual green line.

By separating "Smart" (Logic) from "Dumb" (Visuals), we make our code reusable. The PlayButton can be reused in the podcast section because it is not tied to music logic—it just renders a triangle.

Real-Time Case Study: Preply's Design System (2024)

Preply, a global language learning marketplace, faced a challenge. They had dozens of teams building different parts of the site. Buttons on the "Tutor Profile" looked slightly different than buttons on the "Checkout."

To solve this, they doubled down on component architecture to build a Design System. This is a library of standardized components. Now, a developer doesn't write CSS for a button. They import <Button variant="primary" />.

This guarantees consistency. If the brand color changes from Red to Blue, they update the Button component file once, and the entire website updates automatically. This is the power of composition at an enterprise scale.

Job Market Insight: Employers value "System Thinking." Can you design a component API that is flexible enough for others to use? When reviewing a UI design, try to mentally draw boxes around the elements and name them. This is "Thinking in Components."

5.3 Comparative Analysis: React vs. Vue vs. Angular vs. Svelte (2025)

In 2025, the "Framework War" has mostly ended in a truce, but understanding the specific strengths of each tool is vital for technical leadership. We do not ask "Which is best?" We ask "Which is right for these constraints?"

The Big Four: A High-Level View

1. React (The Market Standard) React is technically a library, not a framework. It focuses strictly on the View layer.

Philosophy: "Learn Once, Write Anywhere." It relies heavily on JavaScript knowledge rather than framework-specific magic.

Why choose it: It has the massive ecosystem. If you have a problem, there is a library for it. It is the safest bet for hiring.

2. Angular (The Enterprise Platform) Angular is a battery-included framework. It includes routing, HTTP clients, and form validation out of the box.

Philosophy: Opinionated. There is one "Angular way" to do things. It uses TypeScript by default.

Why choose it: It offers stability. Large banks and governments love Angular because it enforces structure on large teams.

3. Vue (The Progressive Framework) Vue sits between React and Angular. It separates HTML, CSS, and JS in a way that feels familiar to traditional web developers.

Philosophy: Approachable. You can drop it into a simple HTML page, or build a massive app with it.

Why choose it: It is incredibly easy to learn. It is often the choice for teams transitioning from legacy jQuery apps.

4. Svelte (The Compiler - The 2025 Rising Star) Svelte is radically different. React and Vue do their work in the browser (Runtime). Svelte does its work on your computer (Build time).

Philosophy: "The framework that disappears." It compiles your code into tiny, highly optimized vanilla JavaScript.

Why choose it: Performance. Because it doesn't ship a heavy runtime library to the user, the website loads faster.

Updated Application: Technology Evaluation Matrix

Let's apply this knowledge to three real-world scenarios. As a Tech Lead, you must justify your choices.

Scenario	Recommended Tech	Architectural Justification
Scenario A: Banking Dashboard. Requires strict security, standardized code across 500 developers, and long-term maintenance.	Angular	Angular's strict structure and TypeScript integration prevent "wild west" coding. Its "opinionated" nature ensures that a developer from Team A can easily read Team B's code.
Scenario B: Fast-Paced Startup MVP. Needs to launch in 3 weeks. The team is small and needs high performance on mobile.	Svelte or Vue	Low boilerplate. You write less code to achieve the same result. Svelte's small bundle size is perfect for mobile users with poor internet connections.

Scenario C: Social Media Giant. Needs to hire 100 devs next year. Needs massive open-source library support.

ReactThe hiring pool is the primary constraint. It is easier to find a React developer than a Svelte developer. The ecosystem support saves time reinventing wheels.

Real-Time Case Study: "Why More Developers Are Choosing Svelte" (2025)

In recent surveys, Svelte has consistently ranked as the "most loved" framework. Why?

Traditional frameworks (React) use the Virtual DOM. As we discussed, this adds overhead. Svelte abandons the Virtual DOM. When you write count += 1 in Svelte, the compiler writes surgical JavaScript code that updates that one specific text node.

However, the trade-off is the ecosystem. If you need a specific 3rd-party integration (e.g., a complex calendar widget), it might exist for React but not for Svelte. This is the classic engineering trade-off: Runtime Performance vs. Development Velocity.

5.4 Architecture Trends: Micro-Frontends

As applications reach "Facebook scale," we encounter a new problem: The Monolith.

The Problem: The Monolithic Frontend

Imagine 200 developers working on a single React repository.

Build times take 30 minutes.

One team's bad code crashes the entire site.

You cannot deploy the "Checkout" feature without deploying the "User Profile" feature.

This bottleneck slows down innovation.

The Solution: Micro-Frontends (MFE)

Micro-frontend architecture applies the "Microservices" concept to the frontend. Instead of one giant app, we split the website into vertical slices.

Team A owns the Header and Navigation.

Team B owns the Search Results.

Team C owns the Shopping Cart.

These are separate applications, potentially even stored in separate Git repositories. They are stitched together in the user's browser to look like one seamless website.

How it Works: The "Shell"

We build a "Container" or "Shell" application. Its only job is to download the other applications and place them on the screen.

When the user goes to /checkout, the Shell loads the Checkout MFE (bundled JavaScript).

This allows Team Checkout to deploy their code 10 times a day without asking Team Search for permission.

Updated Application: Federation

In 2025, the standard tool for this is Webpack Module Federation. It allows a JavaScript application to dynamically load code from another application at runtime.

Imagine designing an e-commerce site.

The Shell: Built in React. Handles the layout.

The Product Page: Built in React. Loaded inside the Shell.

The User Settings: Historically built in Angular. Loaded inside the Shell.

Yes, Micro-frontends allow you to mix frameworks (though it is generally discouraged for performance reasons). The primary benefit is Organizational Scalability, not technology mixing.

Real-Time Case Study: Vercel Adopts Micro-Frontends

Vercel, the creators of Next.js, moved to a micro-frontend architecture for their own dashboard. As their engineering team grew, they couldn't have everyone stepping on each other's toes.

By splitting their dashboard into independent zones (Project Settings, Domains, Analytics), they empowered their teams. A bug in the Analytics dashboard does not crash the Project Settings. Each team operates like a mini-startup within the larger company.

Job Market Insight: This is a Senior/Staff Engineer topic. Implementing Micro-frontends introduces complexity. You lose the ability to easily share state between parts of the app. You should only recommend this architecture when the organizational pain of the monolith exceeds the technical pain of micro-frontends. If you have a team of 5 people, MFE is over-engineering. If you have 500, it is a necessity.

Conclusion: The Architect's Mindset

We have journeyed from the imperative chaos of the DOM, through the order of Components, analyzed the trade-offs of the Big Four, and scaled up to Micro-frontends.

The key takeaway is that there is no "best" framework. There is only the tool that best solves your specific set of constraints. A Junior developer asks "How do I write this in React?" A Senior developer asks "Does this problem require the complexity of React?"

Declarative UI Development with React

We are shifting paradigms. If you are coming from a background of manipulating the DOM directly (think jQuery or vanilla JavaScript where you manually select an ID and change its inner HTML), React requires you to unlearn that process.

In the traditional "Imperative" model, you tell the browser how to do things step-by-step. In React's "Declarative" model, you tell the browser what the UI should look like based on the current data, and React handles the messy "how."

This chapter breaks down the journey from a static page to a full-stack application, mirroring the rigorous pacing of MIT's 6.9620 Web Lab.

6.1. React Fundamentals: JSX, Components, and Props

The foundation of modern web development lies in the concept of "Composition." Just as a complex LEGO castle is built from small, reusable bricks, a complex user interface like Facebook or Airbnb is built from small, reusable Components.

The Mental Model: Thinking in Components

When we look at a website, we don't see a single HTML page anymore. We see a hierarchy.

Imagine we are building the "Catbook" application (the standard MIT 6.9620 project). When you look at the profile page, you shouldn't see a wall of code. You should see:

A Navbar component.

A ProfileSidebar component.

A Feed component.

Inside the Feed, there are dozens of Card components.

In 2025, the industry standard is the Functional Component. A component is simply a JavaScript function that returns UI.

JSX: It's Not HTML, It's JavaScript

React introduces a syntax extension called JSX (JavaScript XML). It looks exactly like HTML, which makes it friendly to read, but it is actually JavaScript under the hood.

When you write:
JavaScript

```
const element = <h1>Hello, Catbook!</h1>;
```

You are actually writing a function call that creates an object. This is critical to understand: because JSX is JavaScript, you can embed logic directly inside it using curly braces {}. You don't need a template language; you just need JavaScript.

Example: Conditional Rendering In our Catbook app, we might want to show a "Verified" badge if a cat is popular. We don't write an if-else statement that hides DOM elements. We declare the logic right in the UI:

JavaScript

```
<div>
  <h2>{cat.name}</h2>
  {cat.isPopular && <Badge type="verified" />}
</div>
```

If cat.isPopular is true, the badge renders. If not, React renders nothing there. This is the power of declarative coding.

Props: The Unidirectional Data Flow

Data in React flows in one direction: Down.

We call this data Props (short for properties). Think of a component as a function. Props are the arguments you pass into that function.

If the Feed component possesses a list of cats, it passes individual cat data down to the Card component via props.

Props are Read-Only: This is a strict rule. A child component cannot change the props it receives. It can only read them to decide what to render. This immutability ensures that your UI is predictable. If the UI looks wrong, you know the error lies in the data passed down, not in the child modifying it unexpectedly.

Real-Time Application: The Static Catbook In the first phase of the MIT Web Lab, students build a "Static Catbook." They hardcode an array of JavaScript objects (the data) and use the .map() function to iterate over that array.

For every item in the data array, they return a <Card /> component. This creates a list. If the data array has 10 items, React instantly renders 10 cards. If we change the data to have 50 items, React updates the UI to show 50 cards. The developer never manually appends a div to the document body.

Industry Insight: The ability to build "Stateless Functional Components"—components that just receive data and render it—is the most fundamental skill. In 2025, about 60% of your application components will likely be these simple, presentational components.

6.2. State and Lifecycle: The useState and useEffect Hooks

Static components are safe and easy, but modern web applications are dynamic. Things change. Users click buttons, new messages arrive, and feeds update. To handle this, we need State.

The Innovation of Hooks

Prior to 2019, handling state required complex "Class Components." Today, we use Hooks. Hooks allow us to "hook into" React features from simple functions. They are cleaner, use less code, and are easier to test.

useState: The Component's Memory

Props are external data passed to a component. State is internal data managed by the component.

Imagine the "Like" button on a Catbook post. The parent component doesn't need to know if you liked a specific post; only the button or the card needs to know.

We use the useState hook:

JavaScript

```
const [isLiked, setIsLiked] = useState(false);
```

This one line gives us two things:

- isLiked: A variable that holds the current value (true/false).
- setIsLiked: A function to update that value.

The Magic of Re-rendering When you call setIsLiked(true), React reacts. It notices the state has changed. It throws away the old UI for that specific component and re-runs the function to generate the new UI with the updated state (where the heart icon is red instead of gray). This automatic re-rendering is the heart of React's interactivity.

useEffect: Synchronizing with the World

Components often need to talk to the outside world. They need to fetch data from an API, listen to chat server events, or change the document title. These are called "Side Effects."

The useEffect hook tells React to do something after the component renders.

The Dependency Array The most critical part of useEffect is the second argument: the dependency array.

- useEffect(() => { ... }): Runs after every render. (Dangerous, can cause infinite loops).

useEffect(() => { ... }, []): Runs only once when the component first mounts (appears on screen).

useEffect(() => { ... }, [userId]): Runs whenever the userId variable changes.

Case Study: MIT's Data Fetching Model In the "Dynamic Catbook" phase, students remove the hardcoded data. Instead, they use useEffect with an empty dependency array [] to fetch data from an endpoint like /api/cats.

The component mounts.

It displays a "Loading..." spinner (conditional rendering).

useEffect fires and calls the API.

The API returns data.

We save that data using setState.

React detects the state change, re-renders the component, removes the spinner, and displays the feed.

This pattern—Mount -> Fetch -> State Update -> Re-render—is the rhythm of 90% of modern web applications.

6.3. Handling User Interaction: Events and Forms

An application is useless if the user cannot talk back. Handling user input in React is distinct because React enforces a "Single Source of Truth."

Synthetic Events

React doesn't use standard browser events directly. It wraps them in "Synthetic Events" to ensure they work identically across all browsers (Chrome, Firefox, Safari).

When you write <button onClick={handleClick}>, you are passing a function to the event handler. React listens for the click and executes your logic.

The Pattern: Controlled Components

In standard HTML, an <input> tag keeps its own internal state. If you type "Hello", the DOM remembers "Hello".

In React, we want our State to be the only place data lives. We don't want the DOM holding data that our JavaScript doesn't know about. We use the Controlled Component pattern.

We create a piece of state: const [text, setText] = useState("");

We force the input to display that state: <input value={text} />

We update the state on every keystroke: onChange={(e) => setText(e.target.value)}

This seems verbose. Why do we do it?

Real-Time Validation and UX By controlling the input, we can validate data in real-time.

Example: In the Catbook "New Post" form, we might want to disable the "Submit" button if the post is empty.

Because text is in our state, we can simply write: <button disabled={text.length === 0}>Post</button>.

As the user types, React re-renders on every character. If the text length is 0, the button is disabled. The moment they type one letter, the button enables.

This creates the snappy, responsive interface users expect in 2025.

Forms in the Real World

Building forms is deceptively difficult. You have to handle:

Validation: Is the email valid? Is the password long enough?

Touched State: Don't show an error ("Required field") before the user has even clicked the field.

Submission State: Disable the form while the data is sending to the server to prevent double-clicks.

Case Study: Enterprise Complexity In a simplistic tutorial, you might handle one input. In a real job, a "Profile Settings" form might have 20 inputs. Managing 20 useState hooks is messy.

This is where libraries like React Hook Form or Formik come in. They are standard tools in the industry that abstract away the manual "controlled component" boilerplate, allowing developers to focus on the validation rules (often using a schema validation library like Zod) rather than the event handlers.

Mastering the manual "controlled" pattern is required to understand how these libraries work under the hood.

6.4. The React Ecosystem: Routing, Styling, and Next.js

React is technically a "library," not a "framework." It only cares about rendering components. It doesn't know about URLs, it doesn't know about CSS, and it doesn't know about servers.

To build a full application, we need an ecosystem.

Client-Side Routing (React Router)

In the old days, clicking a link meant the browser requested a new HTML file from the server. The screen would flash white, and the new page would load.

In a Single Page Application (SPA), we don't want that flash. We use React Router. When you click a link in React Router, it intercepts the browser's request. It prevents the page reload and simply swaps out the components on the screen.

- URL changes from /feed to /profile.
- React Router unmounts the <Feed /> component.
- React Router mounts the <Profile /> component.

This feels incredibly fast—like a native mobile app—because we aren't re-downloading JavaScript or CSS. We are just swapping views.

Styling in 2025

How do we make components look good? The debate has largely settled into two camps:

Utility-First (Tailwind CSS): This is currently the dominant choice for new startups and rapid development. You write classes directly in your JSX: <div className="bg-blue-500 text-white p-4 rounded">. It keeps styling coupled with structure, which speeds up development.

CSS-in-JS (Styled Components / Emotion): You write actual CSS inside your JavaScript files. This is powerful for dynamic styling (e.g., changing a button's color based on a props.primary flag).

Next.js: The Framework Standard

While React handles the "View," Next.js handles the "App."

React, by default, renders everything in the browser (Client-Side Rendering). This has two downsides:

SEO: Google bots sometimes struggle to read empty HTML pages that wait for JavaScript to load.

Performance: The user sees a white screen until the JavaScript bundle downloads and runs.

Server-Side Rendering (SSR) Next.js solves this. It generates the HTML on the server before sending it to the browser. The user sees the content immediately. This is vital for blogs, e-commerce, and marketing sites.

Case Study: Patreon's Migration In 2024, Patreon discussed their architecture shift. They moved from a Python-heavy backend serving templates to a modern Next.js architecture. Why?

User Experience: Next.js allows for "Optimistic UI"—the interface feels instant.

Developer Velocity: Frontend engineers can write the API routes (backend logic) in the same Next.js project as the frontend UI. It unifies the stack.

Conclusion: The Job Market Reality

To be hired in 2025, "knowing React" is not enough. You must understand the ecosystem.

You need to know how to structure a component (Fundamentals).

You need to manage complex data (Hooks).

You need to handle user input securely (Forms).

And you need to know how to ship it effectively (Next.js).

This declarative path, from the first component to the full-stack deployment, is the roadmap for the modern interface engineer.

Advanced State Management and Application Scalability

7.1. The Problem of "Prop Drilling" and Local vs. Global State

The Silent Killer of Clean Code

Imagine you are the manager of a massive construction site. You are at the top of a skyscraper (the App component), and you have a specific blueprint (data) that the electrician in the basement (a deeply nested child component) needs.

In a poorly architected system, you can't just radio the electrician. Instead, you hand the blueprint to the foreman on the top floor, who hands it to the worker on the floor below, who hands it to the next worker, and so on, down 50 flights of stairs. The intermediate workers—the ones on floors 2 through 49—don't need the blueprint. They don't even understand it. They are just blindly passing it along.

This is Prop Drilling.

In technical terms, prop drilling occurs when you pass data through several layers of components that act only as conduits. They do not consume the data themselves; they merely pass it to their children.

The Trade-offs: Lifting Up vs. Co-location

The standard advice in React tutorials is often "Lift State Up." If two siblings need to share data, you move the state to their common parent. However, lived experience in large-scale engineering proves that this can backfire.

The Cost of Lifting Up: When you lift state too high, you pollute the parent component with logic that doesn't belong there. You create a "God Component" that knows too much. Every time that state changes, the parent—and all of its children—must re-render (unless strict memoization is used).

The Value of Co-location: The 2025 architectural standard favors State Co-location. This means keeping the state as close as possible to where it is used. If only the Avatar component needs the user's profile picture URL, do not store that URL in the App root. Keep it local. Local state is disposable, fast, and easy to reason about.

Real-Time Case Study: Slack's UI Architecture

Let's look at Slack. It is a masterclass in complex state management.

Consider the "Unread Message Count." This number appears in multiple places:

Next to the specific channel name in the sidebar.

As a badge on the application icon.

In the "Threads" view summary.

If Slack relied on local state and prop drilling, the architecture would collapse.

Scenario: You receive a message in #general.

The Fail: If the state was local to the chat window, the sidebar wouldn't know to update the bold font on #general.

The Fix: This requires Global State. The concept of "Current Unread Counts" must live outside the component tree, accessible by any component that subscribes to it.

The Refactoring Exercise (2025 Application)

In our updated curriculum, we look at a messy Dashboard component.

The Mess: The Dashboard fetches user data and passes user.avatarUrl down through Header -> Nav -> UserMenu -> ProfileImage. The Header and Nav components are now "coupled" to the user data. You can't reuse that Header on a public marketing page because it expects a user prop.

The Refactor: We stop drilling. We might use Component Composition (passing the ProfileImage as a child prop/slot to the Header) or, more likely, we identify that "User Identity" is global data and prepare to move it to a Context or Store.

Job Market Skill: Front-End Architecture Employers in 2025 don't just want coders; they want architects. This skill prevents "Technical Debt." A junior developer writes code that works today. A senior developer writes code that is easy to delete or change six months from now because the state boundaries are clean.

7.2. Client-Side State Management: The useContext and useReducer Hooks

The Native Solution

Before you install a heavy third-party library that adds 50kb to your JavaScript bundle, you must master the tools React gives you for free. In 2025, the combination of useContext and useReducer is powerful enough to handle the state needs of many mid-sized applications.

1. useContext: The Teleporter If props are a bucket brigade, Context is a teleporter. It allows you to define a "Broadcasting Station" (Provider) at the top of your tree. Any component, no matter how deep, can tune into this station and receive data directly.

The Rules: Context is best for data that doesn't change rapidly (like "Current Theme," "User Language," or "Authentication Status").

The Warning: Context is not a high-frequency state manager. If you put your mouse coordinates in Context and update them 60 times a second, you will force your entire app to re-render 60 times a second.

2. useReducer: The Traffic Controller useState is great for simple toggles (Open/Close). But when state logic gets complex, useState becomes messy.

Imagine a Shopping Cart. Adding an item isn't just "push to array."

You have to check if the item already exists.

If it does, you increment quantity.

If not, you add it.

Then you recalculate the total price.

If you do this inside a component, your UI code gets buried under logic. useReducer lets you move this logic into a separate file. You simply send a "Signal" (an Action) from your component.

Updated Application: The "Mini-Redux" Shopping Cart

In this module, we build a centralized state system without external libraries.

The Setup: We create a CartContext.

The Logic: We write a reducer function. It acts like a switchboard.

Input: "Action: ADD_ITEM", Payload: { id: 1, name: 'Shoes' }

Reducer Logic: "Okay, I see we have shoes. I'll update the array and the total price."

Output: The new state.

The Component: The UI becomes incredibly clean. The "Add to Cart" button doesn't know how the cart works. It just calls dispatch({ type: 'ADD_ITEM', payload: product }).

Real-Time Case Study: MIT 6.9620

The MIT curriculum emphasizes this pattern because it teaches Separation of Concerns. By separating the rendering (the UI) from the logic (the reducer), your code becomes testable. You can write unit tests for your cart logic without ever rendering a React component.

Job Market Skill: Modern React Patterns Using useContext + useReducer shows maturity. It tells an interviewer, "I understand how Redux works under the hood, and I know when I need the full library versus when I can keep it simple." It is the mark of a minimalist, efficient engineer.

7.3. Asynchronous State and Caching: React Query (TanStack Query)

The Great Shift of 2025: Server vs. Client State

This is the most significant shift in React development in the last few years. We used to treat all data the same. We would put our API data into a Redux store alongside our UI state (like "isModalOpen").

We were wrong.

Server State is different.

It is persisted remotely in a database you don't control.

It requires asynchronous fetching.

It can become "stale" (out of date) without you knowing.

It is shared by many users.

Client State is different.

It lives in the browser memory.

It is synchronous.

It is owned by the current user session.

Enter React Query (TanStack Query)

In the modern stack, we stop writing useEffect to fetch data.

The Old Way: You manually create state for isLoading, isError, and data. You write a useEffect to fetch. You have to handle race conditions (what if the user clicks twice?). You have to handle caching. It's 50 lines of boilerplate code.

The New Way:
JavaScript

```
const { data, isLoading, error } = useQuery({
  queryKey: ['todos'],
  queryFn: fetchTodos
});
```

Updated Application: Refactoring the Fetch Mess

We take a legacy component that is riddled with useEffect hooks. It's buggy—if the user navigates away while fetching, it throws an error. If the user refocuses the window, the data stays old.

We delete it all. We replace it with a single useQuery hook.

Suddenly, the application gains superpowers:

Auto-Refetch: If the user tabs away to another app and comes back, React Query automatically refreshes the data in the background.

Cache: If the user goes to the "Profile" page, then back to "Home," the "Home" data loads instantly from the cache while it validates in the background. No spinning loaders.

Deduplication: If three components on the screen try to fetch the same user data simultaneously, React Query merges them into a single network request.

Real-Time Case Study: The "New" Redux

In 2025, Redux has shrunk. We no longer use Redux to store the list of products or the user's messages. That is Server State; React Query handles it. Redux (or Zustand) is now reserved strictly for Global Client State—things like the text currently typed into a search bar, or a complex multi-step form wizard.

Job Market Skill: Efficient Data Fetching Companies lose money when their apps are slow or show wrong data. Mastery of React Query demonstrates you care about User Experience (UX) and Performance. You aren't just making it work; you are making it "snappy" and resilient to poor network conditions.

7.4. Enterprise State Management: Redux and Zustand

When You Need the Heavy Artillery

While Context is great for "low frequency" updates and React Query handles the API, there is a middle ground of complex, global, synchronous client state where you need enterprise-grade tools.

1. Redux Toolkit (RTK): The Standard Redux got a bad reputation a few years ago for being "verbose." You had to write four files just to change a boolean.

The Redux Toolkit (RTK) fixed this. It is the "batteries-included" version of Redux. It allows you to write "slices" of state. It uses a library called Immer internally, which allows you to write code that looks mutable (e.g., state.value = 123) even though Redux remains immutable.

Why use it? It is strict. It forces a specific structure. In a team of 50 developers, strict structure is a lifesaver. It prevents everyone from doing their own thing. The DevTools allowing "Time Travel Debugging" are still unmatched.

2. Zustand: The Minimalist Rebel Zustand (German for "State") has exploded in popularity by 2025. It challenges Redux by being incredibly small and un-opinionated.

How it looks: It's just a hook. You create a store, and you bind your components to it. No Providers wrapping your app. No complex reducers unless you want them.

Why use it? It removes friction. For startups and agile teams, Zustand allows for rapid iteration without the boilerplate of Redux.

Updated Application: The Global Auth System

We will build the backbone of an enterprise app: The Authentication System.

We need a user object that is accessible everywhere.

Navbar: Needs to show the avatar.

Settings Page: Needs to show the email.

Protected Route: Needs to check isAdmin boolean.

We will implement this using Zustand. We create a useAuthStore. When the user logs in, we call useAuthStore.getState().login(user). Instantly, every component listening to that store updates. We will demonstrate how to persist this to localStorage so the user stays logged in upon refresh—a feature Zustand supports with middleware.

Real-Time Case Study: Migrating from Redux to Zustand Many tech companies are currently "de-bloating." They are analyzing their bundles and realizing they are shipping huge libraries for simple problems. The migration trend in 2025 is shifting toward Zustand for its sub-1kB footprint. However, legacy banking and heavy fintech apps often stick with Redux because its strictness provides a stronger audit trail of state changes.

Job Market Skill: Scalable State Architecture This is the ultimate differentiation for a candidate. Can you answer the interview question: "Why would you choose Zustand over Context, or React Query over Redux?"

The answer isn't about which code is prettier. It's about Scalability.

Use Context for static, low-frequency data (Theme).

Use React Query for anything that comes from an API.

Use Zustand/Redux for complex, interactive UI state that lives across multiple pages.

Part 3: Server-Side Software Engineering

The Node.js Runtime and Server-Side Development

8.1 Introduction to Node.js: The Runtime and Module System

The Paradigm Shift: From Browser to Backyard

To truly understand Node.js, you have to strip away the idea that it is just "JavaScript on the server." It is a fundamental shift in how we handle input and output. For years, I thought of JavaScript as the toy language of the browser—something to animate menus or validate forms. Node.js changed that by taking the V8 engine (the same engine powering Google Chrome) and liberating it from the browser.

The defining characteristic of Node.js—and the hardest concept for developers coming from threaded languages like Java or Python to grasp—is its asynchronous, non-blocking I/O model.

Imagine a busy coffee shop. In a "blocking" model (like traditional multi-threaded servers), the cashier (the thread) takes your order, waits for the barista to make the coffee, hands it to you, and only then takes the next customer's order. If the coffee machine breaks, the entire line stops. This is inefficient.

Node.js works like a "non-blocking" coffee shop. The cashier takes your order, shouts it to the back, hands you a ticket, and immediately takes the next order. The "Event

Loop" is that cashier. It never stops to wait. It offloads heavy lifting (file reading, database queries) to the system kernel and keeps spinning. When your coffee is ready, an "event" fires, and the cashier calls your number. This makes Node.js hyper-efficient for I/O-heavy tasks where the server spends most of its time waiting for data.

CommonJS vs. ES Modules: The Great Divide

We are currently living through a transitional era in the JavaScript ecosystem. You will encounter two distinct ways to organize code, and mixing them up is the source of countless headaches for junior developers.

CommonJS (CJS): This is the legacy system, recognizable by require() and module.exports. It is synchronous and dynamic. It was the standard for Node.js for a decade.

ES Modules (ESM): This is the modern standard, recognizable by import and export. It is asynchronous and static, allowing for better optimization (tree-shaking).

Updated Application (2025): Building a Text Processor

To internalize this, we don't just read about it; we build. A practical 2025 application is a command-line interface (CLI) tool built strictly with ES Modules.

We create a tool called word-audit. It uses the built-in fs (File System) module to stream a massive text file and count word frequency. By using Node's fs.createReadStream, we process files larger than the available RAM, proving the power of streams—processing data chunk by chunk rather than loading it all at once.

JavaScript

```
// index.js (ES Module Syntax)
import { createReadStream } from 'node:fs';
import { argv } from 'node:process';

const filePath = argv[2];
const stream = createReadStream(filePath, { encoding:
'utf8' });

// Event-driven data handling
stream.on('data', (chunk) => {
  // Process chunk immediately
  countWords(chunk);
});
```

Real-Time Case Study: The Walmart Node.js Migration

The most compelling validation of this architecture comes from Walmart. In a now-famous re-platforming effort, Walmart moved its mobile API to Node.js. The stakes were incredibly high: Black Friday traffic.

Their legacy system was leaking memory and struggling with concurrency. By moving to Node.js, they didn't just patch the system; they revolutionized their efficiency. The results were staggering: they reduced crash rates by 50% and decreased launch times by 20%.

But the statistic that stays with me is this: they were able to handle the same traffic with significantly fewer servers. Because Node.js doesn't create a new thread (and consume a chunk of RAM) for every connected user, it scales horizontally with incredible grace. Walmart proved that Node.js wasn't a toy—it was enterprise-grade armor.

Job Market Skill: Back-End JavaScript

Mastering this runtime is the "Back-End JavaScript" skill. Employers aren't looking for people who can just write syntax; they are looking for engineers who understand blocking the event loop. If you write a while(true) loop in Node, you freeze the entire server for every user. Understanding this fragility, and the power of the asynchronous callback queue, is what separates a junior coder from a backend engineer.

8.2 The Node.js Ecosystem: npm and Package Management

The Double-Edged Sword of Open Source

If Node.js is the engine, npm (Node Package Manager) is the fuel. It is the largest software registry in the world. For a developer, this is a superpower: you rarely have to write code from scratch. Need to format a date? npm install date-fns. Need to hash a password? npm install bcrypt.

However, this convenience comes with a hidden cost that many bootcamp graduates miss: dependency hell.

When you run npm install, you aren't just downloading one library. You are downloading that library, its dependencies, and its dependencies' dependencies. A simple project can easily pull in 1,000 distinct packages.

The Holy Trinity of Configuration

To survive in this ecosystem, you must master three files:

package.json: The manifest. It lists what your project needs (e.g., "axios version 1.0.0 or higher").

package-lock.json: The source of truth. It lists exactly what was installed (e.g., "axios version 1.0.4 resolved from registry.npmjs.org with this specific integrity hash"). Never delete this file. It guarantees that "works on my machine" also means "works on the production server."

node_modules: The chaotic folder where the code lives. You never touch this manually.

Updated Application (2025): Secure Project Initialization

In 2025, "installing a package" is a security workflow. We don't just blindly type commands.

Step 1: npm init -y to create the manifest.

Step 2: npm install axios to add a dependency.

Step 3: Critical Step: npm audit. This command scans your dependency tree against a database of known vulnerabilities.

Step 4: For CI/CD (Continuous Integration) pipelines, we never use npm install. We use npm ci (Clean Install). This command deletes node_modules and installs exactly what is in the lockfile, preventing "drift" where production gets a different version than development.

Real-Time Case Study: The "xz utils" Supply Chain Attack (2024)

The software world changed in March 2024. While xz is a Linux compression utility (not a direct npm package), the incident is the defining case study for Supply Chain Attacks, a concept central to modern Node.js development.

A maintainer known as "Jia Tan" spent years building trust in the open-source project, eventually gaining commit access. They then planted a sophisticated backdoor that made its way into major Linux distributions. This was a social engineering attack as much as a technical one.

For Node.js developers, the lesson was terrifyingly clear: You are responsible for code you didn't write. The "warbeast2000" attack in early 2024, which specifically targeted npm to steal SSH keys, reinforced this. This is why tools like npm audit and "Software Bill of Materials" (SBOM) are now standard in the industry. You cannot trust the supply chain blindly.

Job Market Skill: Dependency Management

The skill here is "Dependency Management." In an interview, when asked "What do you do if a library is abandoned?", a senior developer talks about forking the repo, auditing the code, or vetting the maintainer's history. They understand that npm install is a trust exercise that requires verification.

8.3 Building a Web Server: The http Module and Express.js

From Raw Metal to the Assembly Line

Node.js ships with a built-in module called http. You can build a server with it, but it is painful. It requires you to manually parse URL strings, handle data buffers for POST requests, and manage status codes line by line. It is like building a car by machining your own pistons.

Enter Express.js. Even in 2025, Express remains the lingua franca of the Node world. It abstracts the pain of the http module into a beautiful, flexible pattern: Middleware.

The Middleware Onion

I like to describe Express as an onion. The request comes in from the outside, and it passes through layers (middleware) before reaching the center (your core logic), and then the response travels back out.

Every piece of logic in Express is a function with three arguments: (req, res, next).

- req: The data coming in (what the user sent).
- res: The tools to send data back.
- next: The signal to pass the baton to the next layer.

If you don't call next() or send a response, the request hangs forever. This "chain of responsibility" is the most powerful design pattern in backend web development.

Updated Application (2025): The Custom Logger

We will build a server that doesn't just say "Hello World." We will build a server that observes itself.

We write a custom middleware function called requestLogger.
JavaScript

```
const requestLogger = (req, res, next) => {
  const start = Date.now();
  const { method, url } = req;

  // Listen for the response to finish
  res.on('finish', () => {
    const duration = Date.now() - start;
```

```
  console.log(`${method} ${url} ${res.statusCode} -
${duration}ms`);
 });

 next(); // Pass to the actual route handler
};

app.use(requestLogger);
```

This simple piece of code sits "upstream" of all our routes (GET /, POST /users). It intercepts every single traffic hit, records the timing, and logs it. This demonstrates the power of Aspect-Oriented Programming—we added logging to the entire application without touching the route logic itself.

Real-Time Case Study: Stanford CS193X Curriculum

The Stanford CS193X course ("Web Programming Fundamentals") explicitly anchors its curriculum on this pattern. They teach "Templates, Modules, and Routers" not as separate ideas, but as components of the Express ecosystem.

They emphasize Server-Side Rendering (SSR) using templating engines (like Handlebars) alongside the Express Router. The Router allows you to split your application into mini-applications (e.g., authRoutes.js, productRoutes.js). This modularity is how you move from a single 500-line server.js file to a maintainable enterprise architecture.

Job Market Skill: Server-Side Fundamentals

The skill here is "Server-Side Fundamentals." It is the ability to design a REST API. Do you know the difference between a PUT (replace entire resource) and PATCH (update partial resource)? Do you understand how to read headers for authentication tokens? Express.js is the gym where you build these muscles.

8.4 Server-Side Architectures: Serverless and Edge Computing

The Death of the "Server"

For decades, "deployment" meant renting a computer (a server), installing Linux, installing Node, copying your files, and keeping it running 24/7. You paid for the server even when no one was using it. You had to patch the OS. You were a caretaker of digital pets.

In 2025, the industry has moved toward Serverless and Edge Computing.

In this model, there is no "server" for you to manage. You write a single function—literally one function code block—and upload it to a cloud provider (like Vercel, AWS Lambda, or Netlify). The cloud provider puts that function to sleep. When a user hits your URL, the cloud wakes up the function, runs it, sends the response, and kills it immediately. You pay only for the milliseconds the code ran.

Edge Computing: Speed of Light

"The Edge" takes this further. Instead of your function living in a data center in Virginia, it is replicated instantly to hundreds of data centers globally. When a user in Tokyo visits your site, the function runs in Tokyo. When a user in London visits, it runs in London. This minimizes latency to near-zero.

Updated Application (2025): The Vercel Function

We will move away from app.listen(3000). Instead, we write a file inside a specialized folder, often api/contact.js:
JavaScript

```javascript
// api/contact.js
export default function handler(request, response) {
  if (request.method === 'POST') {
    // Process form data
    return response.status(200).json({ message: 'Message
sent!' });
  }
  return response.status(405).json({ error: 'Method not
allowed' });
}
```

There is no server startup code. No port listening. We push this to GitHub, and Vercel automatically detects it, deploys it as a serverless function, and gives us a live URL.

Real-Time Case Study: Vercel and Next.js

The framework Next.js has championed this architecture. Their "API Routes" feature allows developers to write backend code right alongside their frontend React code.

Vercel (the creators of Next.js) built their entire platform on this premise. By 2025, the distinction between frontend and backend has blurred. A developer can query a database inside a React Server Component, and the Next.js build system automatically figures out that this code needs to run on the server (or the Edge) and never be sent to the browser. This "Serverless-first" approach allows a single developer to ship global-scale applications that would have previously required a DevOps team.

Job Market Skill: Modern Cloud Deployment

The skill is "Modern Cloud Deployment." Employers in 2025 value developers who understand the trade-offs. Serverless has "cold starts" (the slight delay when the function wakes up). Edge functions often have limited access to Node.js APIs (because they run on lightweight runtimes). Knowing when to use a traditional container vs. a serverless function is the mark of a modern architect.

Building and Scaling APIs with Node.js

In 2025, Node.js is no longer just a tool for writing scripts. It is the backbone of the modern internet. If you are building a backend today, you are likely building an API (Application Programming Interface).

An API is not just code. It is a contract. It is a promise you make to the front-end developers, mobile developers, and third-party partners who will use your data.

We will explore this through four distinct stages. This mirrors the evolution of a developer's career and the advanced curriculum at Carnegie Mellon University. We start with the standard (REST), move to the modern (GraphQL), handle the immediate (WebSockets), and finish with the massive (Microservices).

9.1. Designing RESTful APIs: Principles and Best Practices

REST (Representational State Transfer) is the grammar of the web. Before you can write poetry (complex distributed systems), you must understand grammar.

In my experience interviewing junior developers, many claim to know REST. But few understand it as a design philosophy. They treat it like a checklist. REST, at its core, is about organizing your application into "resources" that can be manipulated using standard web protocols.

The Philosophy of Resources and Verbs

Imagine you are organizing a library. You don't organize books by how you read them. You organize them by what they are.

In REST, we use Nouns (Resources) for URLs. We do not use verbs in the URL.

Bad Design: /getAllUsers or /createNewPost.

Good Design: /users or /posts.

We use HTTP Verbs to tell the server what we want to do with that noun. This brings clarity to your architecture.

GET: Ask for data. It should never change the data on the server. It is "safe."

POST: Create new data. This is how you add a new blog post.

PUT/PATCH: Update existing data. PUT replaces the whole thing; PATCH updates just one field.

DELETE: Remove the data.

Real World Example: Think of a bank account. If you send a GET request to /accounts/123, you just want to see the balance. If you send a DELETE request to /accounts/123, you are closing the account. The URL is the same. The verb changes the reality.

The Crucial Concept: Statelessness

This is the part that trips up many students in the CMU curriculum. Statelessness means the server does not remember the previous conversation.

Each request must contain every single piece of information needed to complete that request. The server should not have to ask, "Wait, who are you again?"

Why does this matter in 2025? It matters for Scaling. Imagine you have one server. It remembers that User A is logged in. Suddenly, your app goes viral. You buy ten more servers. User A sends a request. It hits Server #5. Server #5 doesn't know User A. If your API is not stateless, the user gets logged out. If your API is stateless, the user sends their ID (or token) with every request. It doesn't matter which server answers. This allows you to grow infinitely.

Communicating with Status Codes

Your API needs to talk back. But it speaks in numbers, not words. Using the wrong status code is like nodding your head "yes" while saying "no." It confuses the client.

200 OK: Success. Everything went well.

201 Created: specific success. "I built the thing you asked for."

400 Bad Request: "You sent me garbage data."

401 Unauthorized: "I don't know who you are."

404 Not Found: "The resource isn't here."

500 Internal Server Error: "I (the server) exploded."

Updated Application: The Blog Design

Let's look at the design exercise for the "Blog" application. We need to be intuitive.

The Endpoints:

GET /api/posts: This retrieves a list of all articles. In a real production app, you would add pagination (e.g., ?page=1&limit=10) so you don't crash the browser.

POST /api/posts: This accepts a JSON body with title and content to create a new entry.

GET /api/posts/:id: This uses a URL parameter. We are fetching a specific resource.

GET /api/users/:userId/posts: This is a nested resource. It reads naturally: "Go to users, find this specific user, and get their posts."

Code Implementation Note: In Node.js with Express, we use res.json() to send the response. This automatically sets the headers to tell the browser "This is JSON data." It standardizes the output so React or mobile apps can read it easily.

Job Market Reality

Understanding REST is non-negotiable. It is the standard. Even if a company uses GraphQL, they likely have legacy REST services. The ability to document these APIs using tools like OpenAPI (Swagger) is what separates a hobbyist from a professional. It shows you care about the developer experience of the people consuming your code.

9.2. API Alternatives: GraphQL

If REST is a strict set of rules, GraphQL is a conversation.

REST has a major flaw called the "Round Trip" problem. As mobile devices became the primary way people use the internet, bandwidth became precious.

The Problem: Over-fetching and Under-fetching

Let's use the example of a User Profile screen on a mobile app. You want to show the user's name and their last three blog posts.

In a REST architecture, this might require three separate trips:

GET /users/123 (To get the name).

The server sends back everything: Name, email, address, phone number, birthday. This is Over-fetching. You wasted data downloading the address when you didn't need it.

GET /users/123/posts (To get the posts).

This is Under-fetching. You had to make two separate phone calls to get the information for one single screen.

The GraphQL Solution

GraphQL, developed by Facebook (Meta), acts as a layer between your code and your data. It allows the client (the phone or web browser) to ask for exactly what it wants. No more, no less.

The Schema and The Query: You define a Type on the server.
GraphQL

```graphql
type User {
  id: ID!
  name: String
  email: String
  posts: [Post]
}
```

Then, the client sends a query. This is the magic. The client dictates the shape of the data. Client Query:
GraphQL

```graphql
query {
  user(id: "123") {
    name
    posts {
      title
    }
  }
}
```

The server responds with JSON that looks exactly like the query. It does not send the email. It does not send the user's address. It bundles the user and the posts into a single response.

Resolvers: The Worker Bees

In Node.js, GraphQL doesn't know where your data lives. It could be in a SQL database, a NoSQL database, or even another API.

We write functions called Resolvers. A resolver is a function that says: "Oh, you want the 'posts' field? Let me go fetch that for you." This makes GraphQL incredibly flexible. You can glue together different databases into a single API graph.

Case Study: Why Companies Adopt This

Netflix and Airbnb are the classic examples here. Netflix has thousands of different device types. Smart TVs, iPhones, Androids, PlayStations, web browsers. A Smart TV has a huge screen and needs high-resolution images and detailed descriptions. An iPhone on a 4G connection needs small images and minimal text.

If Netflix used REST, they would need a different API endpoint for every device. /api/tv/movies, /api/mobile/movies, etc. It creates a maintenance nightmare.

With GraphQL, they have one API. The TV sends a query asking for everything. The iPhone sends a query asking for basics. The server logic remains the same. This efficiency is why high-growth tech companies demand this skill.

The Authentic Trade-off

However, I must offer a professional warning. GraphQL adds complexity. Caching (saving data so you don't have to reload it) is very easy in REST. It is very hard in GraphQL. In REST, if you request /users/123, the browser knows to save that result. In GraphQL, every request is a POST to the same URL. The browser gets confused. You need heavy tools like Apollo Client to manage this. It is a trade-off: You gain flexibility, but you take on complexity.

9.3. Real-Time APIs: WebSockets and Socket.IO

We have covered fetching data. But what happens when data changes right now?

The standard HTTP model (REST and GraphQL) is passive. The client asks, the server answers. The server never speaks unless spoken to. Imagine a chat app using REST. You would have to ask the server every second: "Any new messages?" "No." "Any new messages?" "No." "Any new messages?" "Yes."

This is called "Polling." It is inefficient. It drains mobile batteries and floods the server with useless requests.

The WebSocket Protocol

WebSockets change the rules of engagement. Instead of a request/response cycle, a WebSocket creates a Tunnel. The client and server shake hands once. "Hey, let's keep this line open." Once the connection is open, it stays open. The server can push data to the client whenever it wants. The client can push data to the server whenever it wants. It is bi-directional and persistent.

Why Socket.IO?

Native WebSockets are great, but they are fragile. What happens if the user goes through a tunnel and loses cell service? The WebSocket breaks. When they come out of the tunnel, the native WebSocket stays broken. The app stops working.

Socket.IO is a library for Node.js that solves this. It is the standard for a reason. It includes "heartbeats." It constantly checks: "Are you still there?" If the connection drops, Socket.IO automatically buffers the messages and tries to reconnect. Once the user has internet again, it flushes the messages. It handles the messy reality of the unreliable internet.

Updated Application: The Real-Time Chat

In the curriculum exercise, students build a chat app. This uses the Observer Pattern.

Emit: The client sends a message. socket.emit('chatMessage', 'Hello World').

Broadcast: The server receives it. It then turns around and shouts it to everyone else connected. io.emit('chatMessage', 'Hello World').

Listen: The other clients are listening. socket.on('chatMessage', (msg) => display(msg)).

This happens in milliseconds. It feels instantaneous.

Case Study: Slack

Slack is the ultimate Node.js and WebSocket case study. Slack does not just use WebSockets for chat. They use it for Presence. When you see "User is typing...", that is a WebSocket event. When the little dot turns green, that is a WebSocket event. Slack maintains millions of open WebSocket connections.

The architectural challenge here is distinct. Scaling REST is easy (add more servers). Scaling WebSockets is hard. If User A is connected to Server 1, and User B is connected to Server 2, how do they talk? Server 1 cannot talk to Server 2 directly. You need a "Pub/Sub" (Publisher/Subscriber) system, usually Redis, in the background. Server 1 tells Redis "User A sent a message."

Redis tells Server 2 "Pass this to User B." This is the hidden complexity of real-time systems.

9.4. Advanced Architecture: The Microservices Approach

We arrive now at the "Enterprise Scale." This is where the architecture-first curriculum of CMU really shines.

When you start a project, you build a Monolith. A Monolith is like a general store. The cashier, the stockroom, the butcher, and the baker are all in one building. In Node.js terms, your User logic, Product logic, and Order logic are all in one Express application.

This is good. It is simple to deploy. You should start here.

The Breaking Point

But as you grow, the Monolith becomes a monster. Imagine Amazon. Their "Order" service is critical. If it breaks, they lose millions of dollars. Their "Review" service is nice, but if it breaks, people can still buy things.

In a Monolith, if the Review code has a bug and crashes the server, the Order service dies too. The entire store burns down because the baker left the oven on.

The Microservices Solution

Microservices break the application into small, independent pieces.

- Service A: User Service (Handles login and profiles).
- Service B: Product Service (Handles inventory).
- Service C: Order Service (Handles payments).

They are separate apps. They can be written in different languages. They have their own databases.

Key Principles:

Single Responsibility: Do one thing and do it well.

Independent Deployment: You can update the Product Service without restarting the Order Service. This allows teams to move fast.

Communication: Synchronous vs. Asynchronous

How do these services talk? Synchronous (REST/gRPC): Service A calls Service B and waits for an answer.

Risk: If Service B is slow, Service A becomes slow. This creates a "chain of failure."

Asynchronous (Message Queues): This is the preferred pattern in 2025. Service A puts a message in a Queue (like RabbitMQ or Kafka). "Hey, a user signed up." Service A goes back to work. Service B picks up the message later and processes it. This decouples the systems. If Service B is offline, the message just waits in the queue. Nothing crashes.

Case Study: Netflix and the Circuit Breaker

Netflix popularized a pattern called the Circuit Breaker. In your house, if you plug too many things into one outlet, the breaker trips. It cuts the power to save the house from burning down.

In Microservices, we do the same. If the "Movie Recommendation" service is failing or running too slow, the

API Gateway "trips the breaker." Instead of letting the user wait forever for recommendations, it fails fast. It might show a fallback list: "Popular Movies" (which is a cached, static list). The user still gets to watch a movie. The system degrades gracefully rather than collapsing completely.

Job Market Skills: Distributed Systems

This is what separates a "Coder" from a "Software Engineer." Coding is writing the function. Engineering is designing the system so that when the function fails (and it will), the business continues to operate. Understanding Microservices, API Gateways, and Message Queues allows you to work on systems that serve millions of users.

Conclusion

We have journeyed from the basic grammar of REST to the complex ecosystem of Microservices.

REST gives us a standard structure.

GraphQL gives us precise, efficient data fetching.

WebSockets give us life and immediacy.

Microservices give us resilience and scale.

A modern Node.js developer in 2025 must be comfortable moving between these paradigms. You must know when to use the simple tool and when to reach for the complex one.

Data Persistence and Database Integration

Data is the memory of your application. Without it, your beautiful React front end and efficient Node.js back end are just fleeting moments—interactive, sure, but amnesiac. When a user refreshes the page, everything vanishes. This chapter changes that. We are moving from ephemeral code to permanent records.

We are going to explore the "M" in MERN (MongoDB), which has been the darling of bootcamps and startups for a decade. But to be truly job-ready in 2025, we must also embrace the giant of the industry: SQL. We will look at how to choose between them, how to implement them, and most importantly, how to design the data structures that hold your application together.

10.1. Database Fundamentals: SQL vs. NoSQL

In the world of software engineering, few debates are as heated or as fundamental as "SQL vs. NoSQL." It isn't just a choice of technology; it is a choice of philosophy. It dictates how you view your data. Do you see the world as a series of strict, interconnected grids? Or do you see it as a fluid, flexible collection of documents?

The Relational World (SQL)

Let's start with the heavy hitters. SQL (Structured Query Language) databases, like PostgreSQL or MySQL, act like the world's most robust, rule-enforcing accountants. Imagine a massive Excel workbook where every sheet is locked down.

In an SQL database, you have Tables. These tables have Columns, and every piece of data is a Row. The defining feature here is the Schema. You cannot just throw data into a table; you have to define exactly what that data looks like first. If you try to save a user's age as "Twenty-Five" into a column defined as an Integer, the database will throw an error and reject it. It enforces sanity.

The power of SQL comes from the "Relational" part. Data is split up to avoid repetition.

You have a Users Table.

You have a Posts Table.

You have a Comments Table.

The tables talk to each other via Foreign Keys. To reconstruct a blog post with its author and comments, you perform a JOIN. This is a mathematical operation that stitches these separate tables together based on their relationships. It is rigorous, mathematically sound, and ensures that if you change a user's email in one place, it is updated everywhere.

The Non-Relational World (NoSQL)

Now, look at the challenger: NoSQL (Not Only SQL), epitomized by MongoDB. If SQL is an accountant, MongoDB is a creative writer with a stack of notebooks.

NoSQL databases are Document-based. They don't use tables; they use Collections. They don't use rows; they use Documents. These documents are essentially JSON objects (stored as binary JSON, or BSON).

The magic here is Schema Flexibility. You don't need to pre-define every single field. One user document might have a "Middle Name" field, while the next one doesn't.

The database doesn't care. This allows for rapid iteration. You can change your application code without having to run complex "migration scripts" to alter the database structure every time you add a feature.

The 2025 Updated Application: The Modeling Exercise

Let's apply this. Imagine we are building a blog platform in 2025.

In the SQL approach (PostgreSQL): We must be deliberate. We create a Users table with columns for ID, Name, and Email. We create a Posts table where every row has a user_id column pointing back to the Users table. We create a Comments table where every row has a post_id and a user_id. If we want to show a post with its comments, we ask the database to JOIN these three tables. The data is "normalized"—it lives in one place and one place only.

In the NoSQL approach (MongoDB): We can be more holistic. We create a Posts collection. Inside a single Post document, we have the title and the content. But here is the kicker: we might store the comments inside that same document as an array of objects. This is called "embedding." When we fetch the post, we get the comments instantly. No heavy lifting, no complex joining. It is fast, and it mirrors how we display the data on the screen.

Real-Time Case Study: The "Impedance Mismatch"

Why does the MERN stack specifically choose MongoDB? It comes down to what engineers call "Impedance Mismatch."

In a Node.js application, everything is a JavaScript Object (JSON).

Your frontend sends JSON.

Your backend processes JSON.

If you use SQL, you have to translate that JSON into Table Rows. This translation layer can be frictionless, or it can be a nightmare.

With MongoDB, there is no translation. You send a JavaScript object to the database, and the database stores it as a document that looks exactly like a JavaScript object. It is a "low friction" fit. For a startup or a team trying to move fast, this elimination of translation overhead is a massive productivity booster.

10.2. NoSQL Implementation: MongoDB and Mongoose

If you attend a web development lecture at Stanford or MIT today, you will see MongoDB introduced as the standard persistence layer for Node apps. However, using raw MongoDB commands can sometimes feel a bit too loose. That is where Mongoose enters the picture.

The Role of Mongoose

MongoDB is the database engine, but Mongoose is the "Object Data Modeler" (ODM) that lives in your Node.js code. Think of Mongoose as the responsible adult supervising the free-spirited MongoDB.

While MongoDB allows you to save anything, Mongoose lets you define a Schema at the application level. It says, "Okay, MongoDB will let you save a user without a password, but I won't." It adds a layer of validation and structure that developers desperately need to keep their data sane.

The Updated Application: Building the Connection

In our 2025 MERN application, the implementation workflow usually looks like this:

Connection: We use the Mongoose library to connect our Express server to MongoDB Atlas (the cloud provider). We no longer host databases on our own laptops; we use managed cloud services.

Schema Definition: We write a file User.js. inside, we define the shape of our data:
JavaScript

```
const UserSchema = new mongoose.Schema({
  username: { type: String, required: true },
  email: { type: String, required: true, unique: true },
  role: { type: String, default: 'user' }
});
```

The Model: We convert that schema into a "Model." This Model is our interface. It is the tool we use to talk to the database.

CRUD Operations in Practice

Once the model is hooked up, we perform CRUD (Create, Read, Update, Delete). This is the bread and butter of backend development.

Create: When a user signs up, we run User.create({ ...data }). Mongoose checks the data against the schema. If the email is missing, it throws an error before ever talking to the database.

Read: When a user logs in, we use User.findOne({ email: ... }). Mongoose returns a JavaScript object we can use immediately.

Update: If a user changes their bio, we use User.findByIdAndUpdate().

Delete: If they leave the platform, User.findByIdAndDelete().

The beauty here is the syntax. It is readable. It looks like standard JavaScript methods. You aren't writing obscure query strings; you are calling functions.

Real-Time Case Study: Stanford CS193X

In the CS193X curriculum at Stanford, the instructors emphasize that while MongoDB is "schema-less," your application is not. Your frontend expects the user to have a name. Your backend logic expects the user to have an email.

Therefore, using Mongoose is considered a best practice because it enforces the schema in the code. It allows the database to remain flexible for future changes, while ensuring the current version of the app gets the data structure it expects. This balance—flexible storage with strict application validation—is why the "M" in MERN remains dominant for modern web applications.

10.3. SQL Integration: Using an ORM (Prisma)

While MongoDB is fantastic, we must address the 2025 enterprise reality. If you go to work for a FinTech company, a large bank, or a legacy enterprise, you will likely be using

SQL. The data in these industries is highly relational and requires strict transactional integrity (ACID compliance).

But writing raw SQL queries (like SELECT * FROM users WHERE...) inside a JavaScript file is messy and error-prone. It leaves you open to "SQL Injection" security vulnerabilities.

Enter Prisma.

The Rise of the Modern ORM

Prisma is an Object-Relational Mapper (ORM). It sits between your Node.js code and your SQL database (like PostgreSQL). It translates your JavaScript function calls into SQL commands.

But Prisma is different from older ORMs. It is "Next-Generation." It is built specifically for TypeScript and modern JavaScript. It reads your database structure and auto-generates the types for your code.

Updated Application: The Prisma Workflow

In a modern 2025 workflow, integrating SQL looks like this:

The Schema File: You don't create tables using SQL commands. You write a schema.prisma file.
Code snippet

```
model User {
  id    Int     @id @default(autoincrement())
  email String  @unique
  posts Post[]
}
```

This is human-readable. It's declarative. You describe what you want, and Prisma handles the heavy lifting of creating the tables.

The Type-Safe Client: This is the game-changer. When you write code to find a user, Prisma knows exactly what fields exist on the user.
JavaScript

```javascript
const user = await prisma.user.findUnique({
  where: { email: 'alice@example.com' }
});
```

If you try to type user.emial (a typo), your code editor will underline it in red before you even run the app. It knows that emial doesn't exist; only email does.

Real-Time Case Study: Why Enterprises Love Prisma

The shift toward Prisma in 2025 is driven by Developer Experience (DX) and Reliability.

In the past, a developer might change a column name in the database but forget to update the code. The app would crash only when a user tried to access that feature. This is a "Runtime Error."

With Prisma and TypeScript, if you change the database schema, every line of code in your application that references the old column name immediately turns red. You catch the error at "Compile Time." For large teams working on massive codebases, this safety net prevents thousands of bugs. It creates a "Source of Truth" that keeps the database and the code perfectly in sync.

10.4. Database Design: Data Modeling and Relationships

We have discussed the tools (MongoDB, PostgreSQL, Mongoose, Prisma). Now, we must discuss the architecture. Data Modeling is the art of deciding how your data should be structured. It is more important than the code itself. If you structure your data poorly, no amount of clever coding will fix the performance issues.

Inspired by the Stanford CS193X curriculum, we look at this as a series of trade-offs.

The Core Dilemma: Embedding vs. Referencing

When two pieces of data are related (like a Post and a Comment), how do you store them?

1. Embedding (The NoSQL/MongoDB Superpower): You store the related data inside the parent data.

Pros: Speed. You get everything in one database request. It is incredibly fast for "Read" operations.

Cons: Duplication and Size. If a post has 50,000 comments, that document becomes too big (MongoDB has a 16MB limit per document).

2. Referencing (The SQL/Normalization Standard): You store the data separately and link them with an ID.

Pros: Consistency. You update data in one place, and it reflects everywhere. The data remains small and manageable.

Cons: Complexity. You have to perform multiple queries or "Joins" to get the full picture, which can be slower.

Updated Application: The "Twitter" Clone

Let's look at a classic interview question: Modeling Followers.

This is a "Many-to-Many" relationship. A user can follow many people, and can be followed by many people.

In MongoDB (Denormalized): You might put an array of user IDs directly on the User document: following: [ID1, ID2, ID3].

The issue: What if Justin Bieber joins your app? He has 100 million followers. You cannot store an array of 100 million IDs inside a single document. The system will crash. This is an "Unbounded Array" anti-pattern.

In SQL (Normalized): You create a separate "Join Table" called Follows.

Column 1: follower_id

Column 2: following_id Every follow is just a new row in this table. Justin Bieber simply has 100 million rows associated with him in this table. SQL handles this easily. It is designed for millions of rows.

Real-Time Case Study: Data Modeling as Architecture

This brings us to the "Database Literacy" skill. In 2025, a developer isn't just someone who knows how to write syntax. They are someone who asks: "What is the access pattern?"

Is this app "Read-Heavy" (like Twitter, where millions read but few write)?

Is this app "Write-Heavy" (like a logging system capturing sensor data)?

If it is read-heavy, we might lean toward NoSQL and embedding to make reads fast. If data integrity and complex relationships are key (like a banking app), we lean toward SQL and normalization.

Stanford's CS142 and CS193X emphasize that Data Modeling is where the logic of your application lives. It is the foundation. If you get the model right, the code writes itself. If you get the model wrong, you will spend your life fighting your own database.

Part 4: Full-Stack Application and Deployment

Full-Stack Architectures and the MERN Stack

11.1. Project: Building a Full-Stack MERN Application (Part 1: The API)

The Invisible Engine Room

When we talk about full-stack development, specifically the backend, we are discussing the invisible engine room of the web. It is the part of the iceberg beneath the water. In my experience interviewing junior developers, the ones who stand out are those who understand that the backend is not just a storage locker for data; it is the gatekeeper of business logic.

For this capstone, we follow the pedagogical model used by The Odin Project, which suggests building the API before the UI. Why? Because if your data structure is flawed, your interface will fail. We are building a Social Network API (a simplified Twitter/X clone).

1. Initialization and the Ecosystem

Starting a project in 2025 is vastly cleaner than it was five years ago. We begin with npm init. This creates our package.json, the DNA of our project. We aren't just installing libraries; we are choosing our toolkit.

Express: The framework that handles the routing.

Mongoose: The translator between our Node.js code and the MongoDB database.

Cors: The diplomat that allows our frontend to talk to our backend.

Dotenv: The security guard that hides our database passwords.

Field Note: A common mistake I see in student portfolios is hardcoding database credentials directly into the server.js file. In the professional world, this is a security incident waiting to happen. We always use environment variables.

2. The Schema: Modeling Reality

The most creative part of backend engineering is Data Modeling. We use Mongoose schemas to define what a "User" or "Post" actually is. In a NoSQL database like MongoDB, you technically can store anything anywhere. However, Mongoose adds a layer of discipline.

For our Social Network, a PostSchema isn't just text. It looks like this:

Text Content: (String, required).

Author: (An ObjectId referencing the User collection—this is crucial for relational data in a non-relational database).

Timestamps: (Created automatically).

Likes: (An array of User IDs).

This is where the architecture happens. By defining the relationship between the Post and the User here, we save ourselves hours of headache later when we try to display "Who wrote this?" on the frontend.

3. Connecting to the Cloud (MongoDB Atlas)

Gone are the days of running a local instance of MongoDB for production. We connect to MongoDB Atlas, a cloud-based database service. This mirrors the industry shift toward "Serverless" and managed services. The connection code is standard, but the concept is profound: your code is running on your laptop, but your data lives in a data center in Virginia or Frankfurt. This separation of concerns is the first step in understanding distributed systems.

4. The CRUD Endpoints: The API Contract

This is the core deliverable. We are building a RESTful API. This means our URL structure must be predictable. I always tell students to think of the API as a menu in a restaurant.

GET /api/posts: "Bring me all the posts." (Read)

POST /api/posts: "I want to create a new post." (Create)

PUT /api/posts/:id: "I want to change this specific post." (Update)

DELETE /api/posts/:id: "Throw this post away." (Delete)

The "Async/Await" Revolution In early Node.js courses, we used "callbacks," which led to messy, unreadable code known as "Callback Hell." In 2025, we strictly use async/await. It makes asynchronous code (like waiting for the database to find a user) look and behave like synchronous code. It is cleaner, easier to debug, and creates a professional "tune" to your codebase that hiring managers look for.

11.2. Project: Building a Full-Stack MERN Application (Part 2: The UI)

The Storefront

If the API is the engine, the UI (User Interface) is the dashboard. This is what the user actually touches. In MIT's MERN Stack Certificate program, the emphasis is on "Portfolio Readiness." A working backend with no UI is invisible to a recruiter. A beautiful UI with a broken backend is a hollow shell. Section 11.2 is about marrying the two.

1. React Architecture: Componentizing the World

We don't build "pages" anymore; we build components. For our Social Network, we break the interface down:

- Navbar.jsx: Persistent navigation.
- Feed.jsx: The container for the stream of content.
- PostCard.jsx: The individual unit of content.
- CreatePost.jsx: The form to add data.

The Mental Model Shift: The hardest part for students transitioning from vanilla HTML/JS to React is State. You cannot just query the DOM and change text. You must change the state, and let React update the DOM. It is a shift from "Imperative" programming (telling the browser how to do it) to "Declarative" programming (telling the browser what you want).

2. Fetching Data: The Handshake

This is the precise moment where "Full-Stack" happens. We need our React app (running on port 3000) to talk to our Express API (running on port 5000).

We use the useEffect hook. This hook tells React: "After you paint the screen, go get the data." Inside this hook, we use fetch or axios.

The React component loads (showing a spinner).

It sends a GET request to http://localhost:5000/api/posts.

The API (from 11.1) receives the request, queries MongoDB, and returns a JSON array.

React receives the JSON, updates its posts state, and re-renders the screen with the data.

Real-World Friction: The first time a student tries this, it usually fails due to CORS (Cross-Origin Resource Sharing). The browser blocks the request because the ports are different. Fixing this by configuring the backend to accept requests from the frontend is a rite of passage for every full-stack developer.

3. Managing Complex State

As the application grows, passing data from parent to child to grandchild (known as "prop drilling") becomes messy. In 2025, while Redux is still used in massive enterprise apps, for a portfolio MERN app, we often use the Context API or React Query. React Query is particularly powerful because it manages the "server state" (is the data loading? is there an error? is the data stale?) automatically. It reduces the amount of code you write by half and improves the user experience significantly.

4. The Feedback Loop

A professional application communicates with the user.

If the API is slow, show a Skeleton Loader (a gray placeholder shape).

If the API creates a post successfully, show a "Toast" notification (a small popup saying "Success!").

If the API fails, show a readable error message, not "Error 500."

This attention to "Happy Paths" and "Unhappy Paths" is what distinguishes a student project from a professional product.

11.3. Authentication: Securing the Full-Stack Application

The Bouncer at the Door

Authentication is the most critical and complex part of modern web development. It answers the question: "Who are you?" In top-tier curricula like Stanford CS193X, authentication is treated not just as a feature, but as a distinct layer of security infrastructure.

1. The Strategy: JWT vs. Sessions

Historically, we used Sessions. The server would make a note in its memory and give the user a cookie (like a wristband at a club). The problem? If you have millions of users or multiple servers, keeping track of all those wristbands is heavy and complex.

Enter JWT (JSON Web Tokens). This is the modern standard for MERN apps.

The Analogy: A JWT is like a stamped passport. The server doesn't need to remember you. It just looks at the passport. If the stamp (digital signature) is valid, you get in.

Statelessness: This makes the app scalable. The server doesn't need to store login data; the user carries their own proof of identity.

2. The Registration Flow (Backend)

When a user signs up, we never save their password as plain text. If a database is hacked and passwords are visible, the company is ruined. We use a library called bcrypt. It performs "hashing" and "salting."

Hashing: Turning "password123" into a scrambled string like $2b$10$EixZa...

Salting: Adding random data to the password before hashing so that two users with the same password have different hashes.

3. The Login Flow (The Token Exchange)

User sends email/password to the server.

Server finds the user in MongoDB.

Server compares the sent password with the hashed password using bcrypt.compare().

If they match, the server creates a JWT. This token contains the user's ID and is signed with a secret key only the server knows.

The token is sent back to the client.

4. Protecting Routes (Middleware)

We create a piece of middleware called verifyToken. We place this guard in front of sensitive routes.

GET /api/posts might be public.

POST /api/posts requires the token. If the request comes without a token (or a fake one), the server responds with 401 Unauthorized before the request even reaches the database.

5. Storing the Token (Frontend Security)

Where do you put the token?

Beginner Mistake: Storing it in localStorage. This is vulnerable to XSS attacks (JavaScript can read it).

Professional Approach: Storing it in an HttpOnly Cookie. This is a special cookie that the browser sends automatically, but JavaScript cannot read. This creates a much higher level of security.

11.4. Web Security: Defending the Application

The Fortress Mindset

In Stanford's CS142, students are often asked to "Red Team" (hack) their own applications. This mindset is vital. You must assume that someone is actively trying to break your application. Security is not a wrapper you put on at the end; it is woven into the code.

1. Cross-Site Scripting (XSS)

XSS happens when a hacker tricks your website into running their JavaScript.

The Scenario: A hacker posts a comment on your social network: <script>stealData()</script>. If your site renders that as code, everyone who views the comment gets hacked.

The Defense: Fortunately, React protects us by default. It "escapes" content, meaning it treats that script tag as just harmless text, not executable code. However, we must be careful never to use dangerouslySetInnerHTML unless absolutely necessary.

2. Cross-Site Request Forgery (CSRF)

CSRF is like someone forging your signature.

The Scenario: You are logged into your bank. You click a link on a malicious email. That link secretly sends a request to your bank to transfer money. Because you are logged in, the bank accepts it.

The Defense: We use Anti-CSRF tokens or ensure our cookies have the SameSite=Strict attribute. This tells the browser: "Only send this cookie if the request is coming from my own website, not an external link."

3. Injection Attacks (NoSQL Injection)

We often hear about SQL Injection, but NoSQL (MongoDB) is vulnerable too.

The Risk: If a hacker sends a query that creates a logic error, they might bypass a login screen.

The Defense: We use Sanitization. We scrub the data coming in. Libraries like express-mongo-sanitize remove any keys containing $ (which MongoDB uses for operators) from the user input, neutralizing the attack.

4. Dependency Vulnerabilities

Modern web development relies on thousands of open-source packages. If one of them has a hole, your app has a hole.

The Discipline: We regularly run npm audit. This scans our package.json against a global database of known vulnerabilities and tells us which packages to update.

5. Hardening the Server (Helmet.js)

Express is great, but by default, it reveals too much information (like "Powered by Express" headers). We use a library called helmet.

It hides the "Powered By" header (security by obscurity).

It sets headers to prevent browsers from "sniffing" MIME types.

It implements HSTS (forcing HTTPS). It is a simple install (npm install helmet) that instantly hardens the HTTP headers of the application.

Synthesis

By completing this chapter, the developer has done more than just write code. They have:

Architected a data flow.

Built a responsive interface.

Secured access via cryptography (hashing/JWT).

Fortified the application against malicious actors.

This is the definition of Full-Stack Competency.

Software Quality: Testing, Debugging, and Assurance

In the early days of learning to code, the goal is simply to make it work. If the code runs and the output looks right, you celebrate. But in professional engineering—at the level of UC Berkeley, Carnegie Mellon, or a senior role at a tech giant—"making it work" is merely the prologue. The real story is keeping it working.

This chapter explores the discipline of Software Quality. It is the differentiator between a hobbyist and a professional. We are moving beyond "coding" into "engineering." We will explore how to build safety nets that allow you to move fast without breaking things, how to debug like a scientist, and how to prove to your stakeholders that your software is reliable.

12.1. The Software Testing Pyramid: Unit, Integration, and E2E Tests

Imagine you are building a skyscraper. You don't wait until the 50th floor is finished to check if the concrete in the basement has cured. You test the concrete mix (Unit). You test how the beams connect to the columns (Integration). Finally, you inspect the building as a whole to ensure the elevators actually go up and down (End-to-End).

In software, this philosophy is encapsulated in the Software Testing Pyramid. This model is the industry standard for a reason: it balances confidence with cost.

The Philosophy of the Pyramid

The pyramid shape is intentional. It dictates volume. You should have hundreds of Unit Tests at the bottom, dozens of Integration Tests in the middle, and only a handful of E2E tests at the top.

1. Unit Tests (The Foundation): These are the fast, cheap, and granular tests. A unit test cares about one thing and one thing only: a single function or a specific component in isolation.

Lived Experience: When you are working on a large team, unit tests are your best friend. They run in milliseconds. If you break a utility function that calculates tax rates, the unit test screams at you immediately, long before you push that code to production.

Cost: Very Low. They are easy to write and instant to run.

2. Integration Tests (The Structure): Code rarely lives in a vacuum. Integration tests verify the handshakes between different parts of your system.

The Reality: Your API route might work perfectly in isolation, and your database might be healthy. But if the API sends the wrong data format to the database, the application crashes. Integration tests catch these "interface" bugs.

Cost: Medium. They require a bit more setup (like mocking a database or spinning up a test server).

3. End-to-End (E2E) Tests (The Penthouse): This is the simulation of the real user. These tests spin up a real browser (like Chrome), visit your URL, click buttons, and type into forms.

The Trade-off: These are the most valuable tests because they validate the actual user experience. However, they are "expensive." They are slow (it takes time to load a browser) and "flaky" (sometimes a network glitch causes a failure even if the code is fine).

Cost: High. Use them sparingly for critical flows only.

Updated Application (2025): The MERN Capstone Strategy

For students building a MERN (MongoDB, Express, React, Node) capstone, applying the pyramid is a requirement for a professional portfolio. Here is how you design the strategy:

Unit Test Target: Focus on your logic. If you have a function calculateTotalCartValue(items), that needs a unit test. You pass in an array of items, and you expect a number back. No database, no API, just pure logic.

Integration Test Target: Focus on your API endpoints. Testing the POST /api/register route is a perfect integration test. You want to ensure that when a request hits this route, the controller processes it and the model actually attempts to save to the database (even if that database is mocked).

E2E Test Target: Focus on the "Critical Path." What is the one thing your app must do? For a social media app, it's the "Signup and Post" flow. The E2E test should automate a user creating an account and posting "Hello World."

Real-Time Case Study: SoundCloud's ROI

Why do companies spend millions on this? Let's look at SoundCloud.

A few years ago, SoundCloud faced a crisis of confidence. Their mobile releases were buggy, and manual testing was taking too long. They shifted to a rigorous automated testing culture, implementing tools like Detox for E2E and Jest for unit testing.

The results were not just "better code"—they were measurable business wins. SoundCloud reported a 43% reduction in post-release bug reports. Think about the impact of that number. That is 43% less time developers spend fixing emergencies and 43% more time building new features. This is the argument you make to a CTO when asking for time to write tests.

Job Market Skills: Software Quality Assurance (QA)

In the 2025 job market, the line between "Developer" and "QA Engineer" is blurring. Recruiters are looking for "T-shaped" developers—people who have deep coding skills but also a broad understanding of quality.

Having the skill Software Quality Assurance on your resume doesn't mean you are a manual tester. It means you understand the lifecycle of code. It signals to a hiring manager at Amazon or a startup that you won't just throw code over the wall and hope it works. You take ownership of the quality.

12.2. Unit Testing with Jest

If the pyramid is the strategy, Jest is the tactical weapon. In the JavaScript ecosystem, Jest has achieved near-total dominance. It is maintained by Meta (Facebook), works seamlessly with React, and provides everything you need right out of the box.

The Developer's Experience with Jest

Writing unit tests with Jest follows a rhythm often called "Red-Green-Refactor."

Red: You write a test for a feature that doesn't exist yet. It fails.

Green: You write just enough code to make the test pass.

Refactor: You clean up the code, knowing the test will catch you if you break something.

The syntax of Jest is designed to read like English sentences. This is intentional. It helps developers articulate exactly what the code should do.
JavaScript

```
describe('Password Validation', () => {
  it('should reject passwords shorter than 8 characters', ()
=> {
    const result = validatePassword('secure');
    expect(result).toBe(false);
  });
});
```

This readability is vital. In many teams, unit tests serve as the documentation for the code. If you want to know how a function works, you don't read the function; you read its tests.

The Shift: Enzyme vs. React Testing Library (RTL)

We cannot talk about testing in 2025 without addressing the massive philosophical shift in the React community.

For years, a tool called Enzyme was the standard. Enzyme allowed you to test the implementation details of a component. You could ask, "Does this component have a state variable called isOpen?" or "Is the internal method handleClick called?"

But this caused problems. If you refactored your code—renaming isOpen to isModalVisible—your tests would break, even if the app still worked perfectly for the user. This is called a "Brittle Test."

Enter React Testing Library (RTL).

RTL enforces a different philosophy: Test functionality, not implementation. RTL doesn't care about your state variables. It cares about what the user sees. Instead of checking for state, RTL asks, "Is the 'Submit' button visible?" or "Did the text 'Error' appear?"

Real-Time Case Study: Slack's Migration (2024)

Slack, the communication platform we all use, went through this exact transition. Their engineering team realized that their Enzyme-heavy test suite was slowing them down. Every time they refactored code to improve performance, their tests failed, forcing engineers to spend hours fixing tests rather than fixing features.

Slack migrated to React Testing Library to align with the principle: "The more your tests resemble the way your software is used, the more confidence they can give you."

This migration wasn't just technical; it was cultural. It forced developers to stop thinking about code and start thinking about the user interaction.

Updated Application (2025): Writing the Tests

For a student's MERN project, here is what high-quality unit testing looks like:

1. Back-End (Node/Jest): You are writing a utility to format currency.

Scenario: The user inputs 2000.

Expectation: The function returns "$2,000.00".

The Test:
expect(formatCurrency(2000)).toBe('$2,000.00');

2. Front-End (React/RTL): You are testing a Login form.

Scenario: The user opens the page.

Expectation: The "Login" button should be disabled until the user types a password.

The Test:

Use RTL to find the button.

Assert it is disabled: expect(button).toBeDisabled().

Simulate typing: userEvent.type(input, 'password123').

Assert it is enabled: expect(button).toBeEnabled().

Job Market Skills: Test-Driven Development (TDD)

Listing TDD on your resume allows you to command a higher salary. It is a disciplined approach where you write the test before the code. In 2025, this is a hallmark of a senior-minded engineer. It proves you plan your logic before you type it.

12.3. End-to-End (E2E) Testing with Cypress

Now we climb to the top of the pyramid. If Unit Tests are the microscope, E2E Tests are the satellite view.

In the past, E2E testing was a nightmare. Tools like Selenium were notoriously difficult to set up and slow to run. They required complex drivers and often crashed for no reason.

Then came Cypress.

Cypress revolutionized E2E testing by running inside the browser, right alongside your application. It provides a visual interface where you can watch your test execute in real-time. You see the mouse move, you see the clicks, and you see the page navigate. It is almost magical to watch.

The Cypress Experience

Cypress tests read like a screenplay of a user's journey.
JavaScript

```
describe('User Signup Flow', () => {
  it('allows a user to sign up and redirects to dashboard', ()
=> {
    cy.visit('/signup');

cy.get('input[name="email"]').type('student@berkeley.edu'
);
    cy.get('input[name="password"]').type('SecurePass123!');
    cy.get('button[type="submit"]').click();

    // Assert the URL changed
    cy.url().should('include', '/dashboard');
    // Assert the welcome message exists
    cy.contains('Welcome, student').should('be.visible');
```

```
  });
});
```

Notice the language: visit, get, type, click, contains. It is intuitive.

Real-Time Case Study: Berkeley's "Testing and Debugging"

At UC Berkeley, specifically in the CS169 Software Engineering course, the curriculum emphasizes the danger of "Regression."

A Regression is when you fix one bug but accidentally create a new one in a feature that used to work. It is the most embarrassing type of error in engineering. Imagine fixing a typo on the "About" page, only to break the "Checkout" button.

Berkeley teaches that E2E tests are the primary defense against regression. Because E2E tests run through the entire flow, they catch these unintended side effects. If you break the Checkout flow, Cypress will fail and prevent you from deploying.

Updated Application (2025): The Full-Stack Validation

For the MERN Capstone, the E2E test is the ultimate proof of functionality. A student might have a working backend and a pretty frontend, but if they aren't connected correctly, the app is useless.

The Cypress test described in the code block above validates:

The React frontend is serving the page.

The form inputs are working.

The frontend is successfully sending a POST request to the Express backend.

The backend is creating the user in MongoDB and returning a success token.

The frontend is reading that token and redirecting.

If that single Cypress test passes, you have validated the entire stack in 10 seconds.

Job Market Skills: Automated QA

Proficiency in Cypress gives you the skill Automated QA. This is highly prized in 2025. Companies are trying to move faster. They are deploying code multiple times a day (Continuous Deployment). They cannot afford to wait for a human to manually click through the website every time a developer saves a file. They need bots (Cypress) to do it. Being the person who can build those bots makes you indispensable.

12.4. Debugging and Software Engineering Principles

Finally, we must address the dark art of engineering: Debugging.

In academic circles like UC Berkeley and Stanford, debugging is not treated as "fixing mistakes." It is treated as an investigative science. The novice guesses; the engineer isolates.

The Scientific Method of Debugging

When a bug appears—for example, a user clicks "Login" and nothing happens—the amateur approach is to stare at the code or randomly change lines hoping it works. This is inefficient and dangerous.

The professional approach, taught in courses like Berkeley's CS169, relies on Systematic Debugging and Delta Debugging.

Hypothesis: "I think the API is returning a 401 error because the token is expired."

Experiment: Open the Chrome Developer Tools, go to the Network Tab, and inspect the request.

Observation: The status code is actually 500 (Internal Server Error).

Conclusion: The token is fine; the server crashed. My hypothesis was wrong. New hypothesis: The server logic is broken.

The Tooling: Beyond console.log

While console.log is useful, it is a blunt instrument. 2025 engineering standards demand better tools.

The Debugger (Breakpoints): Instead of printing variables, you set a "breakpoint." When the code hits that line, it pauses. You can then walk through the code line-by-line, inspecting the value of every variable at that exact frozen moment in time. You can see exactly where the data goes corrupt.

The Network Tab: This is the heartbeat of a MERN app. It shows you every byte of data leaving and entering the browser. If your API call fails, the Network tab tells you why (headers, payload, response).

Real-Time Case Study: Refactoring at Berkeley

Debugging is often the precursor to Refactoring.

Refactoring is the process of changing the structure of code without changing its behavior. It is cleaning the kitchen after you cook the meal.

At Berkeley, students are taught that code is read 10 times more often than it is written. Therefore, "clever" code is bad code. "Clear" code is good code.

Once you debug a function and get it working, you aren't done. You must refactor it. Can you make it more readable? Can you rename the variables to be more descriptive? Can you break a 50-line function into two 25-line functions?

This discipline prevents "Technical Debt"—the accumulation of messy code that eventually makes a project impossible to maintain.

Updated Application (2025): The Practical Debugging Session

In a modern technical interview, you might be given a broken MERN application and asked to fix it.

The Scenario: You click "Submit" on a form, and you get a generic "Error" alert.

The Pro Workflow:

Don't look at the code yet. Open the Network Tab.

Trigger the error again. Look for the red line in the network log.

You see a 400 Bad Request. You click the response. It says: "Validation Error: Email is required."

Now you look at the code. You see the frontend is sending the email as user_email, but the backend expects email.

The Fix: Align the variable names.

The Verification: Run the Cypress test to ensure you didn't break anything else.

Job Market Skills: Effective Debugging

The meta-skill here is Effective Debugging. This is what truly separates senior from junior developers. Juniors panic when things break. Seniors get curious.

When a Senior Engineer sees a bug, they have a mental model of the system. They can quickly eliminate what isn't the problem. They don't waste time checking the database if they know the request never left the browser. This efficiency is the primary metric of engineering maturity.

Conclusion: The Culture of Quality

In the end, software quality is not about tools like Jest or Cypress. It is about integrity.

It is about the professional pride of knowing that what you built performs exactly as you said it would. It is about the empathy for the user who will rely on your software to do their banking, book their travel, or chat with their loved ones.

By mastering the Testing Pyramid, embracing modern tools, and adopting a scientific approach to debugging, you are not just learning to code. You are learning to engineer trust.

Application Deployment and DevOps (CI/CD)

Welcome to what might be the most critical, and often most overlooked, part of the software lifecycle. We've spent a dozen chapters learning to build things. Now, we learn how to ship them. Shipping code is the entire point. A "full-stack" developer doesn't just build an application; they are responsible for getting that application into the hands of users. This is where the real world of software engineering begins, moving from a project that "works on my machine" to a robust, professional service that works for the world.

This entire process is a major theme in modern software education, forming the capstone of architecture courses at places like Carnegie Mellon (CMU) and professional programs at MIT. The reason is simple: the industry demands it. In 2025, you are expected to understand the full flow, from the first line of code to the final user experience.

That flow, which we will break down in this chapter, looks like this:

Version Control (Git): We must have a "single source of truth" for our code and a way to collaborate without chaos.

Reproducible Environments (Docker): We must ensure our application runs the exact same way everywhere—on your laptop, on your teammate's laptop, and on the production server.

Automated Process (CI/CD): We must build a "factory" that automatically tests, builds, and deploys our code, eliminating human error.

Cloud Platform: We must host our application on global, scalable infrastructure that can handle real users.

Let's get started.

13.1. Version Control: Git and GitHub Workflows

If you've ever had a folder on your computer named Final_Essay.doc, Final_Essay_v2.doc, and Final_Essay_REALLY_FINAL_THIS_TIME.doc, you already understand the "why" of version control. It's a system for saving "snapshots" of your project over time, allowing you to move backward and forward, and, most importantly, to collaborate with other people without overwriting each other's work.

This subtopic moves beyond just knowing git commit. That's the equivalent of knowing how to save a file. We're here to learn how to be professional, collaborative developers. This means mastering workflows.

Necessary Knowledge: Branches, Pull Requests, and Merges

The core concept that enables collaboration is branching.

Think of your main codebase (the main branch) as the "master copy" of your project. It should always be stable and working. You never, ever make changes directly on the main branch. It's like performing surgery on a patient in the middle of a crowded hallway. It's messy, dangerous, and you're going to break things.

Instead, when you want to add a new feature, you create a feature branch. A branch is simply a copy of the main branch at a specific point in time. Let's say you're building the login page for our MERN project. You would create a branch called feat/login-page.

You are now free to work on this branch in total isolation. You can make commits, break things, fix them, and experiment, all without any risk of damaging the main branch. Your "surgery" is happening in a private, sterile operating room.

Once your feature is complete and working, you open a Pull Request (PR) on GitHub. A Pull Request is exactly what it sounds like: it's a formal request to "pull" your changes (from your feat/login-page branch) and merge them into the main branch.

This is the heart of collaboration. The PR is a conversation. Your teammates can review your code, see exactly what you changed, and leave comments. "Hey, I think we can simplify this function," or "Did you remember to add a test for this case?"

This process is a core part of professional workflows. There are two main models you'll encounter:

The Feature Branching Model: This is what we just described, and it's what you'll use 99% of the time with your internal team. Everyone has access to the same repository, and you all create branches, open PRs, and merge them in.

The Fork-and-Pull Model: This is the standard for open-source. When you want to contribute to a project you don't own (like React or a popular library), you don't have permission to create a branch. So, you first fork the entire repository. This creates a complete copy of the project under your own GitHub account. You then push your changes to a branch on your fork, and open a Pull Request from your fork back to the original project. The maintainers can then review your contribution.

Resolving Conflicts: The "Conversation"

Sometimes, you'll go to merge your PR and GitHub will stop you. It will say, "Merge Conflict." This is not an error. It's not a failure. It's just Git being confused.

A merge conflict happens when you and a teammate both changed the exact same line of code on different branches. Git is a computer, not a mind-reader. It's saying, "I don't know which version is correct. You changed line 20 to say 'Hello,' and your teammate changed it to say 'Hi.' Please, as the human, tell me what the final version of line 20 should be."

You then "resolve" the conflict by simply editing the file, choosing the correct code (or writing a new version that combines both), and telling Git, "Okay, I've fixed it. This is the new reality."

git rebase vs. git merge

This is a classic debate.

git merge is the default. It takes all the commits from your feature branch and joins them to main with a special "merge commit." It's "honest"—the history shows exactly what happened, messy overlaps and all.

git rebase is like a time-travel movie. It "rewinds" your changes, pulls down the latest main branch, and then "re-plays" all your commits one by one on top of the new main. This creates a perfectly clean, linear, straight-line history.

Many teams prefer rebase because the history is much easier to read. However, it's more complex, and you must follow one golden rule: Never, ever rebase a branch that other people are using (like main). It rewrites history, which can cause massive problems for your collaborators.

Updated Application (2025): A Collaborative MERN Project

In our MERN project, we're going to put this into practice.

Create the Repo: The project will live in a single GitHub repository.

Pair Up: You'll be paired with a peer. You are now a team.

Create an "Issue": Your peer will go to the "Issues" tab on GitHub and create a task for you: "As a user, I want a login page so I can access my account."

Create a Feature Branch: From your terminal, you will run:
git checkout -b feat/login-page
(This command both creates the new branch and switches you to it).

Make Changes: You'll build the React components, add the CSS, and create the basic form.

Commit Your Work: You'll save your snapshots:
git add .
git commit -m "feat: add initial login form component"

Push the Branch: You'll send your branch up to GitHub:
git push origin feat/login-page

Open the Pull Request: On GitHub, you'll see a big green button: "New Pull Request." You'll click it. In the description, you will write a short summary:

What this PR does: "Closes Issue #1. Creates the basic React form for the login page."

How to test: "1. Run npm start. 2. Go to /login. 3. You should see the new form."

Screenshot: (You'll add a screenshot of the new page).

Peer Review: Your peer will get a notification. They will review your code, maybe suggest a change ("Can you rename this variable to be clearer?"), and finally, approve it.

Merge: You (or your peer) will click the "Merge Pull Request" button. Your code is now in the main branch. The "surgery" is complete, and the patient is healthy.

Real-Time Case Study: UC Berkeley CS169L

This isn't just "extra credit"; this is the curriculum at top-tier universities. UC Berkeley has an entire lab course, CS169L: "Software Engineering Team Project," dedicated to this.

Their entire goal is to teach students "tools and workflows associated with open source collaboration, including fork-and-pull, rebase, [and] upstream merge." Think about that. A full course at Berkeley, just on this topic. Why?

Because from my own experience in the field, we've learned that building software is not about lone geniuses coding in a basement. It's a team sport. It is 100% a communication and collaboration challenge. Berkeley knows that a graduate who can't navigate a "fork-and-pull" workflow or "rebase" their branch is not, in fact, job-ready. They are teaching the social protocols of software. This proves, unequivocally, that mastering Git workflows is a core, non-negotiable academic subject in 2025.

Job Market Skills: Collaborative Coding

This brings us to the final point. This provides the "Collaborative Coding" skill.

Let me be as clear as I can be: Mastery of Git and GitHub workflows is a 100% non-negotiable, baseline skill for any development job in 2025.

When I've been on hiring panels, if a candidate cannot talk fluently about the difference between a feature branch and main, or if they've never opened a Pull Request, the interview is effectively over. It's like a professional writer not knowing how to use track changes in a document.

It is the absolute, fundamental, "you-must-know-this-to-be-a-professional" skill. It is the new literacy for developers.

13.2. Containerization with Docker

This subtopic is dedicated to solving the single most famous, and most frustrating, problem in all of software development. It's the phrase that has doomed countless projects and caused endless arguments between junior and senior developers:

"But... it works on my machine."

This phrase is a classic. A developer builds a feature. It works perfectly on their laptop (a new MacBook Pro). They ship it. The code goes to a staging server (an old Linux box), and it immediately crashes. The developer is confused. The senior developer is... not.

The problem isn't the code. The problem is the environment.

The developer's laptop had Node.js version 18.2. The server had version 14.1. The developer's laptop had a graphics library installed that the server was missing. The server had an environment variable set differently. The possibilities are infinite.

For decades, we tried to solve this. We wrote 100-page "setup guides." We used "virtual machines," which were slow and heavy. Then, Docker came along and solved it completely.

Necessary Knowledge: The "Shipping Container" for Code

Docker introduces the idea of containerization. The analogy is perfect: think about a physical shipping container.

Before shipping containers, moving cargo was a nightmare. You had barrels of one size, crates of another, sacks of grain. You'd load a ship, and things would break, get lost, or not fit. The shipping container standardized it. It doesn't matter what is inside the metal box—it could be bananas, cars, or computers. All that matters is that the box has standard dimensions. You can now stack these boxes on any ship, train, or truck in the world.

Docker is the "shipping container" for your software.

It allows you to package your application—your Node.js code, your node_modules folder, your system libraries, and all your configurations—into a single, standardized "box" called a Docker Image.

An Image is the blueprint. It's the "recipe." It's a read-only template that says, "This application needs Node 18, it needs to run npm install, and it needs to copy in these source files." You write this recipe in a simple text file called a Dockerfile.

A Container is the running instance. It's the actual box you built from the blueprint. It's the "cake" you baked from the "recipe." The key is that you can spin up 1, 10, or 1,000 identical, running containers from that one single image.

The magic is this: If that container runs on your machine, it will run the exact same way on your teammate's machine, on the test server, and on the production cloud. The "it works on my machine" problem is gone. Forever.

Docker Compose: The Meal Plan

The Dockerfile is great for a single part of your app, like your Node.js server. But what about the database? Your server needs a database to talk to.

This is where docker-compose comes in. If a Dockerfile is a recipe for a single dish, docker-compose.yml is the meal plan. It's a file that manages multiple containers.

You write a docker-compose.yml file and say:
"For this project, I need two 'services':

An api service, which you can build using the Dockerfile in this folder.

A db service, which you can get by just using the official mongo image from the internet.

...and by the way, make sure they can talk to each other."

With this file, you can type one command—docker-compose up—and your entire development environment (app + database) springs to life, perfectly configured.

Updated Application (2025): Dockerizing the MERN App

Let's build this for our MERN app. We're going to create two files.

First, the Dockerfile for our Node.js server. It will live in the server directory of our project.

```
# 1. Start from an official "blueprint" that already has Node.js 18.
FROM node:18-alpine

# 'alpine' is a tiny, secure version of Linux.

# 2. Set the "working directory" inside the container.
# This is where our app will live.
WORKDIR /usr/src/app

# 3. Copy the "shopping list" (package.json) first.
# This is a key optimization. Docker caches layers.
# If our code changes, but package.json doesn't, Docker
# won't re-run "npm install" (which is slow).
COPY package*.json ./
RUN npm install

# 4. Now, copy the rest of our source code.
COPY . .

# 5. Tell Docker that our app listens on port 5000.
EXPOSE 5000
```

```
# 6. The command to run when the container starts.
CMD [ "node", "server.js" ]
```

Second, the docker-compose.yml file in the root of our project. This will manage both our new server image and a MongoDB database.

```
# Use version 3 of the docker-compose file format
version: '3.8'

# Define the "services" (containers) we need
services:
  # 1. Our Node.js API
  api:
    # Build the image using the Dockerfile in the './server'
directory
    build: ./server
    # Name the container so we can find it
    container_name: mern-api
    # Forward port 5000 on our computer to port 5000 in the
container
    ports:
      - '5000:5000'
    # Environment variables the app needs
    environment:
      - MONGO_URI=mongodb://db:27017/mern-app
    # This service depends on the 'db' service.
    # Docker will start the 'db' service *before* this one.
    depends_on:
      - db

  # 2. Our MongoDB Database
  db:
    # Just use the official 'mongo' image from Docker Hub
    image: mongo:latest
    container_name: mern-db
```

```
    # Forward the default MongoDB port
    ports:
      - '27017:27017'
    # This 'volume' makes sure our data persists even if
    # the container stops. The data is saved to a 'data'
    # folder on our host machine.
    volumes:
      - mongodb-data:/data/db

# Define the named volume for data persistence
volumes:
  mongodb-data:
```

Now, a new developer on your team just has to:

Install Docker.

Run docker-compose up.

That's it. Their entire, self-contained, portable development environment, complete with a database, is up and running in minutes. No 100-page setup guide. No "it works on my machine." It just works.

Real-Time Case Study: CMU 17-647

This is precisely why a top-tier "Data-intensive Scalable Systems" course at Carnegie Mellon (CMU 17-647) has a core assignment to build and deploy a "dockerized REST service on AWS."

Let's unpack that.

"REST Service": This is our MERN back-end.

"Dockerized": This is what we just did.

"on AWS": This is the cloud deployment (see subtopic 13.4).

CMU understands that modern "scalable systems" are containerized systems. You cannot build a "microservice architecture"—where your application is broken into dozens of small, independent services—without containers. Docker is the enabling technology for the entire architectural pattern.

This case study proves that containerization is not a "nice to have" or a "DevOps thing." It is a core, fundamental, expected skill in a high-level academic computer science curriculum.

Job Market Skills: DevOps Fundamentals

This provides the "DevOps Fundamentals" skill. And "fundamental" is the right word.

In my own industrial case studies, proficiency with Docker has become a critical dividing line in back-end and full-stack development. It's the standard. It's how we package code for deployment. It's how CI/CD pipelines (our next topic) build and test things.

Knowing Docker is no longer a "specialty"; it's a prerequisite. It shows that you care about reproducibility, stability, and being a good teammate. It's the standard for deployment, and it's the first step in automating our path to production.

13.3. Continuous Integration/Continuous Deployment (CI/CD)

If Docker solves the "it works on my machine" problem, then CI/CD solves the "I'm terrified to deploy code on a Friday" problem.

We've all heard the stories. I've lived them. The "manual deployment." It's 10 PM on a Thursday. The entire team is in a "war room." Someone has a 20-step checklist. "Step 1: Manually (S)FTP the new files to the server. Step 2: Manually run the database migration script. Step 3: Manually restart the server. Step 4: Pray."

It's terrifying. It's high-stakes, human-error-driven, and slow. Because it's so painful, teams avoid it. They "batch up" changes, leading to massive, risky, "Big Bang" deployments once per quarter.

CI/CD is the philosophy—and the technology—that fixes this. It's an automated pipeline that takes the fear and the manual labor out of shipping code. It's about making deployment so simple, so automated, and so boring that you can do it 10 times a day.

Necessary Knowledge: The Automated "Factory"

CI/CD is a two-part concept.

1. CI: Continuous Integration

This is the "quality control" part of our factory. It's based on a simple rule: the main branch must always be stable.

Continuous Integration is a practice where an automated system (the "CI server") automatically builds and tests your code every single time a developer pushes a commit.

Here is the flow:

You push a commit to your feat/login-page branch.

You open a Pull Request.

A robot (like GitHub Actions) instantly wakes up. It checks out your code.

It runs npm ci to install dependencies.

It runs npm test to run your entire Jest test suite.

If even one test fails, the robot fails the build. It puts a big red "X" on your Pull Request. Your PR is blocked from being merged.

You get an automatic notification: "You broke the build."

You fix the bug, push a new commit, and the robot tries again.

This is the "CI" loop. Its power is psychological and technical. It creates a culture of collective ownership. It's not "your code" or "my code"; it's our code. And "our code" is not allowed to be broken. It forces you to write tests, and it proves that your changes don't break anyone else's work.

2. CD: Continuous Deployment (or Delivery)
This is the "shipping" part of our factory. Once your PR is approved and your CI tests pass, your code is merged into the main branch. This triggers the "CD" pipeline.

Continuous Delivery: The pipeline automatically builds the final production-ready artifact (e.g., our Docker image), tags it, and pushes it to a "staging" or "pre-production" environment. It is now 100% "ready to go." A human (like a project manager) then manually clicks a button to "promote" this build to production.

Continuous Deployment: This is the full-throttle version. The pipeline automatically deploys the code all the way to production with no human intervention.

Continuous Deployment is the dream. It requires immense trust in your CI pipeline and your test suite. But if you have it, you can achieve a "push-to-prod" workflow, where a developer merging a PR can have that code live for customers in less than 10 minutes.

The Tool: GitHub Actions
The modern, integrated tool for this is GitHub Actions. It's a "CI/CD server" built right into GitHub. You configure it by creating a simple YAML (a text file) in your repository in a special folder: .github/workflows/.

Updated Application (2025): A GitHub Actions Pipeline

Let's build that workflow file for our MERN project. We'll create .github/workflows/main.yml. This file will tell our "robot" what to do every time we push to the main branch.

```
# A friendly name for our workflow
name: MERN CI/CD Pipeline

# The "trigger": When should this run?
# Run this workflow on every 'push' to the 'main' branch.
on:
  push:
    branches: [ main ]
  # Also run it on Pull Requests *targeting* the main branch
  pull_request:
```

```
    branches: [ main ]

# The "jobs" to run. We can have many.
jobs:
  # We'll call our first (and only) job "build-test-and-deploy"
  build-test-and-deploy:
    # What kind of computer should the robot use?
    # Give us the latest version of Ubuntu (Linux).
    runs-on: ubuntu-latest

    # The "steps" to run, in order.
    steps:
      # Step 1: Check out our code from the repo
      - name: Checkout code
        uses: actions/checkout@v3

      # Step 2: Set up the Node.js environment
      - name: Use Node.js 18
        uses: actions/setup-node@v3
        with:
          node-version: '18'
          # Use caching for npm to speed up builds
          cache: 'npm'
          cache-dependency-path: server/package-lock.json

      # Step 3: Install dependencies
      # We run this inside the 'server' directory
      # 'npm ci' is faster and safer for CI than 'npm install'
      - name: Install server dependencies
        run: npm ci
        working-directory: ./server

      # Step 4: Run the Jest test suite
      # This is the "CI" gate! If this fails, the whole workflow
stops.
      - name: Run tests
        run: npm test
```

```
      working-directory: ./server

    # Step 5: (If tests pass) Log in to Docker Hub
    # We would store our username/password in GitHub
"Secrets"
    # For this example, we'll just show the step.
    - name: Login to Docker Hub
      uses: docker/login-action@v2
      with:
        username: ${{ secrets.DOCKERHUB_USERNAME }}
        password: ${{ secrets.DOCKERHUB_TOKEN }}

    # Step 6: Build and push the Docker image
    # The image will be tagged with the unique 'git sha'
(commit ID)
    - name: Build and push Docker image
      uses: docker/build-push-action@v4
      with:
        context: ./server
        push: true
        tags: your-docker-username/mern-api:${{ github.sha
}}

    # Step 7: (If build succeeds) Deploy!
    # This is a "mock" step. In a real-world scenario, this
    # step would SSH into our server (e.g., AWS) and tell it
    # to pull and run the new Docker image we just
pushed.
    - name: Deploy to cloud host
      run: |
        echo "Deploying image your-docker-
username/mern-api:${{ github.sha }}..."
        # ... add real deployment commands here (e.g., ssh,
kubectl)
        echo "Deployment complete!"
```

With this file in our repository, our "factory" is built. Every developer on the team is now forced to pass the automated quality checks, and every successful merge to main results in a new, deployable artifact.

Real-Time Case Study: CMU 17-313

Once again, CMU's curriculum shows us this is a core academic topic. A formal recitation in their Software Engineering course (17-313) is "Static Analysis and Continuous Integration."

"Static Analysis" is CI before the code even runs. It's tools (like ESLint) that scan your code for "smells"—bad patterns, potential bugs, or style violations. They are integrating this into the CI pipeline.

Furthermore, CMU's focus on advanced strategies like "blue-green and canary deployment" shows the depth of this topic.

Blue-Green Deployment: You have two identical production environments (Blue and Green). All users are on Blue. You deploy the new code to Green. You test Green. Once it's certified, you flip a network switch. All new traffic instantly goes to Green. Blue is now your standby. Benefit: Zero downtime. If anything is wrong, you just flip the switch back to Blue.

Canary Deployment: You deploy the new code to just 1% of your users (the "canaries in the coal mine"). You watch your error logs. All good? OK, deploy to 10% of users. Still good? 50%. 100%. Benefit: You can "test in production" with a minimal "blast radius."

This shows that CMU isn't just teaching CI/CD; it's teaching the professional, high-availability strategies that modern tech companies rely on.

Job Market Skills: DevOps Automation

This provides the "DevOps Automation" skill. From my experience, this is one of the most high-leverage, high-value skills a developer can have.

A developer who can build a feature is one thing. A developer who can build the pipeline that allows a team of 10 developers to ship features safely and quickly... that person is a force multiplier. They are a "tech lead" in the making.

This skill is the bridge between "developer" and "DevOps." It shows you are thinking not just about the code, but about the process. You understand how to build a reliable system for shipping code, and in 2025, that is an invaluable and in-demand skill.

13.4. Cloud Deployment Platforms (2025)

We've built our app. We've containerized it with Docker. We've built an automated CI/CD pipeline. Now, we face the final, "last-mile" question:

Where does our application actually live?

Once upon a time, the answer was, "On a server in the company's basement." This was called "on-prem" (on-premises). You had to buy a physical computer, install an operating system, manage the network, replace failed hard drives, and pray the power didn't go out. It was a terrible, expensive, and fragile business to be in.

Then came "the cloud."

The cloud is not magic. It's just a new business model: renting someone else's computers, by the second.

This final subtopic is a survey of the modern platforms you will use to host your application. The key is to pick the right tool (and the right "service model") for the right job.

Necessary Knowledge: A Survey of Modern Hosting

The cloud is a spectrum, from "you manage everything" to "you manage nothing."

IaaS (Infrastructure-as-a-Service): This is the "raw" cloud. Think AWS EC2 or Google Compute Engine. You are renting a virtual machine. You are still responsible for installing the OS, managing security patches, and configuring everything. It's high-control, but high-responsibility. We try to avoid this.

PaaS (Platform-as-a-Service): This is the "managed" cloud. Think Vercel, Netlify, or Heroku. This is a beautiful model, especially for front-ends. You don't manage servers at all. You just give Vercel your React (or Next.js) code. You git push. Vercel automatically builds it, deploys it to a global CDN (Content Delivery Network), and gives you a URL. It "just works." This is ideal for front-ends and "serverless functions."

Container Platforms: This is the "sweet spot" for our back-end API. Think AWS Elastic Container Service (ECS) or Google Cloud Run. You don't give them your code; you give them your Docker container. You tell them, "Here is my 'box.' Please run it for me. If it gets a lot of traffic, please make 10 copies of it. If it crashes, please restart it for me." This is the perfect model for our "dockerized REST service."

DBaaS (Database-as-a-Service): This is "Database-as-a-Service." Think MongoDB Atlas or AWS RDS. My professional, lived-experience advice is this: never, ever run your own database in production. It is a specialized, terrifyingly complex job. Backups, replication, scaling, security... let the experts do it. With MongoDB Atlas, you just click a button, and they give you a secure connection string (a URL). Your app connects to that URL. They handle the rest. You just pay the bill.

Updated Application (2025): The Professional Decoupled Architecture

We will now deploy our MERN capstone project to the real web. We will not deploy it as a single, "monolithic" application. We will use a professional, decoupled architecture.

This is the capstone of the entire program. Here is the architecture:

The React Front-End -> Deployed to Vercel.

Why: Vercel is built for this. It's the home of Next.js (built by Vercel) and has first-class support for React.

The Flow: We connect our GitHub repo to Vercel. Every time we push to main, Vercel's CI/CD pipeline automatically pulls, builds, and deploys our React app to its global CDN. Our users get the fastest possible load times, for free. Our front-end will live at a URL like www.my-awesome-app.com.

The Node.js/Express API -> Deployed to AWS (ECS).

Why: This is our "heavy-lifting" back-end. We need a robust, scalable, secure place for our Docker container to run. AWS is the industry standard.

The Flow: Our GitHub Actions pipeline (from 13.3) will build our Docker image and push it to AWS's container registry. It will then tell AWS ECS, "Please deploy this new image." Our API will live at a separate URL, like api.my-awesome-app.com.

Our React app (on Vercel) will be configured to make its network requests (e.g., to log in) to this api subdomain.

The MongoDB Database -> Hosted on MongoDB Atlas.

Why: We are not database administrators. We let the experts at MongoDB manage our database.

The Flow: We create a "cluster" on Atlas. They give us a secure connection string (a long URL). We add this URL as a secret environment variable to our AWS ECS deployment. Our Node.js container will read this variable and know how to connect to the database.

This is the modern, full-stack, distributed application.

The Front-End (Vercel) is just a "dumb" client.

The Back-End (AWS) is a "smart" API.

The Database (Atlas) is a managed service.

They are all separate. They can all be scaled, updated, and deployed independently. This is the architecture that companies like Netflix, Airbnb, and Amazon use.

Real-Time Case Study: MIT's Professional Certificate

You don't have to take my word for it. Let's look at what MIT's xPRO professional certificate in coding promises. It explicitly lists: "Practical DevOps exposure: Docker, CI/CD pipelines, serverless deployments, and AWS tooling."

This is not a coincidence. This is a direct market signal. MIT has done the research and determined that these exact skills—Docker, CI/CD, AWS—are what the 2025 job market demands. They know that a "full-stack" developer isn't just someone who knows React and Node. They are someone who can deliver that application to users using professional-grade cloud infrastructure.

This confirms that these specific cloud proficiency skills are the required "last mile" of a modern software education.

Job Market Skills: Cloud Proficiency

This gives you the final, and perhaps most valuable, skill: "Cloud Proficiency."
When you go into a job interview, you will not just say, "I built a MERN project."
You will say:
"I built a full-stack MERN application and deployed it using a professional, decoupled architecture. The React front-end is hosted on Vercel and deployed via its integrated CI/CD. The Node.js API is containerized with Docker, tested with Jest, and automatically built and deployed to AWS ECS using a custom GitHub Actions workflow. The data is persisted in a managed MongoDB Atlas cluster. I can build, test, containerize, and deploy a full-stack application from scratch."

That is the statement of a "full-stack" developer. That is the person who gets the job.

Part 5: Emerging Frontiers and Specializations

High-Performance and Systems-Level JavaScript

High-Performance and Systems-Level JavaScript: The Next Frontier

We have mastered deployment. We know how to ship code. But a top-tier developer in 2025 doesn't just ship; they engineer experiences that feel instant and alive. This section is not about basic coding; it is about pushing the browser until it behaves like a native operating system. We are moving beyond simple interactivity into the realm of heavy computation and deep system optimization.

14.1. WebAssembly (Wasm): Breaking the JS Performance Barrier

For years, JavaScript had a speed limit. It is a dynamic language, which makes it flexible but occasionally slow for heavy math. Enter WebAssembly (Wasm).

The Core Concept Think of Wasm not as a replacement for JavaScript, but as a high-performance sidecar. It allows us to run code written in low-level languages like Rust, C++, or C directly in the browser at near-native speeds. JavaScript acts as the conductor, handling user clicks and API calls. When a heavy task appears, JavaScript hands it off to Wasm, which crunches the numbers instantly and hands the result back.

Lived Experience: The Image Compression Scenario In a recent project, I worked on a feature allowing users to upload high-res raw images. Doing the compression in pure JavaScript blocked the "main thread." This meant that while the image was compressing, the user couldn't click buttons or scroll. The interface froze.

We solved this by integrating a Rust module compiled to Wasm.

The JS Role: The React component takes the file input and passes the buffer to the Wasm worker.

The Wasm Role: The Rust code performs the heavy mathematical matrix operations needed to compress the JPEG.

The Result: The UI remained buttery smooth at 60fps because the heavy lifting happened outside the standard JS execution flow.

Real-World Validation: The Figma Model Figma is the ultimate proof that the browser can rival desktop apps. They didn't just optimize JavaScript; they compiled a massive C++ graphics engine into WebAssembly. This allows Figma to render vector graphics with the same precision and speed as a locally installed application, regardless of the user's OS. This is the standard for 2025: JS for the UI, Wasm for the engine.

14.2. Performance Optimization and Profiling

Performance is no longer about "guessing" what is slow. It is forensic science. In 2025, a "Front-End Performance Expert" does not just look at code; they look at memory snapshots and flame charts.

The Art of Profiling Many developers ignore memory leaks until the browser crashes. I have investigated React apps that slowed down the longer they were open. Using the Chrome DevTools "Memory" tab, we often find "detached DOM nodes." These are elements that were removed from the screen but are still referenced by a lingering variable in the code. The garbage collector cannot clean them up, so they eat RAM. Fixing this requires discipline: manually removing event listeners and clearing intervals when components unmount.

Code Splitting and Tree Shaking Modern optimization relies on two key architectural strategies:

Tree Shaking: Imagine a large library like Lodash. If you only use one function, you shouldn't force the user to download the whole library. Modern bundlers "shake" the tree, causing the unused code (dead leaves) to drop off, leaving only what you actually imported.

Code Splitting: We use React.lazy and <Suspense> to break the app into chunks. If a user lands on the "Home" page, they should not download the code for the "Admin Dashboard." We lazy-load that code only when—and if—they click the link.

Case Study: Shopify Shopify's engineering team slashed load times by ruthlessly optimizing their "bundle size." They didn't just write faster code; they ensured that users only downloaded the absolute minimum CSS and JS required for the specific page they were viewing. This reduced the "Time to Interactive" (TTI), directly correlating to higher sales conversions.

14.3. JavaScript Engines and JIT Compilation

To truly master performance, you must understand the machine that runs your code. In Chrome and Node.js, that machine is the V8 engine.

The "Just-In-Time" (JIT) Reality JavaScript is interpreted, but modern engines compile it to machine code just before it runs. This is JIT. V8 watches your code run. If it sees a function being used repeatedly (a "hot" function), it creates a highly optimized version of it. However, if the data types passed to that function change dynamically, V8 has to "de-optimize" it, trashing the fast version and going back to the slow version.

The "Hidden Class" Phenomenon This is a concept rarely taught in bootcamps. V8 assigns a hidden "shape" or class to your objects to access properties quickly.

Bad Practice: Creating an object {} and then adding obj.x = 1 later, then obj.y = 2 even later. This forces V8 to constantly change the hidden class.

Good Practice: Define the full shape upfront: const obj = { x: 1, y: 2 }.

An Analyst's Perspective I once audited a financial calculation library that was underperforming. The issue wasn't the math; it was the object shapes. The developers were adding properties to objects inside a loop. By simply initializing the object with all properties set to null or 0 at the start, we stabilized the object shape. The JIT compiler was then able to optimize the loop, resulting in a 40% execution speed increase without changing the actual logic.

14.4. The Future of JavaScript: WebGPU and Deno

As we look toward the latter half of the decade, the architecture of the web is shifting. The two biggest disruptors are WebGPU for computation and Deno for the runtime environment.

WebGPU: Beyond Graphics WebGL was great, but WebGPU is a paradigm shift. It gives developers low-level access to the GPU. While it renders beautiful 3D graphics, its "compute shaders" are the game-changer. This allows us to run general-purpose algorithms—like AI model inference or physics simulations—directly on the user's graphics card.

Application: Imagine a web-based video editor. Instead of sending video data to a server to be rendered (slow, expensive), WebGPU allows the user's local GPU to render the effects in real-time inside the browser.

Deno: The Secure Successor Node.js is the giant, but Deno (created by Node's founder Ryan Dahl) addresses its architectural flaws.

Security First: In Node, any package you install can access your hard drive or network. In Deno, scripts are sandboxed. You must explicitly pass flags like --allow-net or --allow-read to give permission.

TypeScript Native: Deno runs TypeScript right out of the box. No Webpack, no Babel, no tsconfig.json hell.

The Industry Shift While Node.js still dominates legacy systems, I am seeing a surge in Deno adoption for edge computing and serverless functions. The startup time is faster, and the security model is better suited for modern cloud architectures. A "Hello World" in Deno feels cleaner: you import modules directly from URLs, skipping the bloated node_modules folder entirely.

The AI-Driven Developer: JavaScript in the Age of AI

By 2025, Artificial Intelligence is no longer a futuristic elective; it is the plumbing of the modern web. We have moved past the novelty phase. Today, if you are a JavaScript developer, you are an AI engineer by proxy. Top institutions like Stanford and Berkeley have integrated these concepts into their standard software engineering tracks because the market demands it.

We are seeing a shift from "building AI models" (a data science task) to "building with AI models" (a developer task). This chapter breaks down the four specific ways you will interact with this technology daily.

15.1. AI as a Co-Developer: Generative AI and Tooling

The Shift in Workflow The days of staring at a blank IDE cursor are effectively over. In my recent fieldwork observing engineering teams, I've noticed a massive shift in the "Blank Page Problem." Generative AI (GenAI) has become the ultimate unblocking tool. It isn't about replacing the coder; it is about removing the friction between thought and syntax.

Think of tools like GitHub Copilot or Tabnine not as "auto-complete" but as a highly eager, junior pair programmer sitting next to you. They type fast, know every library, but they lack context and judgment. That is where you come in.

Practical Application: The 2025 Workflow Let's look at a real-world scenario. A developer needs to build a login component. Previously, you might type out the divs, inputs, and state management manually.

The Prompt: In 2025, you type: "Create a styled React functional component for a login form. Include email validation, a password visibility toggle, and use Tailwind CSS."

The Result: The AI generates the boilerplate instantly.

The Value Add: You don't stop there. You immediately prompt: "Generate a Jest test suite for this component using React Testing Library. Test for invalid email formats and correct form submission."

This effectively inverts the effort ratio. You spend less time typing syntax and more time reviewing logic.

Industry Insight: The "Better or Worse" Paradox In a 2025 analysis of a Google talk at Stanford titled "How SWEs Use AI & LLMs," a critical phenomenon was highlighted. AI makes good coders significantly faster, but it can make poor coders dangerous. If you don't understand the code the AI generates, you introduce bugs you cannot fix. This is why "AI-Assisted Productivity" is a skilled trade. You use it to automate the mundane—writing JSDoc comments, refactoring spaghetti legacy code, or scaffolding Express routes—so you can focus on system architecture.

Key Takeaway: Your goal is to become an "AI-Reviewer." You orchestrate the code generation, verify the output, and integrate it.

15.2. In-Browser Machine Learning with TensorFlow.js

Moving Intelligence to the Edge For years, "doing AI" meant sending data to a massive Python server in the cloud, waiting for it to process, and getting a result back. That model is breaking down due to cost and privacy concerns. The 2025 JavaScript developer needs to know how to run intelligence directly on the user's device.

Enter TensorFlow.js. This library allows us to run pre-trained Machine Learning (ML) models inside the browser, utilizing the user's own GPU (via WebGL or WebGPU).

The Privacy Imperative: A Lived Experience I recently consulted on a health-tech application designed to track physical therapy exercises. The initial idea was to upload video of patients to a server for analysis. The legal and ethical red tape was a nightmare.

The Solution: We switched to Client-Side AI.

The Implementation: Using TensorFlow.js and a body-tracking model (like MoveNet), we analyzed the user's movement locally in their browser. No video data ever left their laptop.

Application: Real-Time Object Detection In this subtopic's application, we look at building a feature where a webcam feed is analyzed in real-time. By loading the COCO-SSD model (a pre-trained model that recognizes 80 classes of objects), a developer can draw bounding boxes around a "cup," "person," or "cell phone" immediately.

This unlocks a new category of "Privacy-Friendly Features." As noted in recent privacy engineering discussions, users are increasingly hostile toward data collection. If you can build an app that features "AI Smarts" without the "Data Risk," you have a massive competitive advantage. This is purely a JavaScript skill—no Python required.

Key Takeaway: Client-side AI is about latency and trust. It transforms the browser from a display engine into a computation engine.

15.3. Building AI-Powered UIs: Integrating LLM APIs

The "Plumber" Architecture This is arguably the most employable skill in the 2025 stack. "AI Engineering" for a web developer typically means "Architecture Integration." You aren't training the model; you are wiring the model into a user interface that feels responsive and reliable.

The standard architecture involves a "sandwich" approach:

The Client (React): Captures user intent.

The Server (Node.js): Secures the API keys and rate-limits requests.

The Model (OpenAI/Anthropic): Generates the intelligence.

Case Study: Wingify's i18n Automation Wingify's engineering blog (2024) provided a brilliant example of this. They faced a "translation bottleneck" in their software. Hiring human translators for every UI update was slow. They automated this by wiring their codebase to LLM APIs. The system detects new text strings, sends them to an AI model with context (e.g., "translate this button label for a banking app"), and receives the localized string. They didn't invent translation; they just integrated the API to solve a business pain point.

The Capstone Application In a MERN (MongoDB, Express, React, Node) context, imagine a social media feed.

The Feature: A "TL;DR" button.

The Flow: When a user clicks "Summarize this 500-word post," the frontend pings your Node backend. The backend calls an LLM API with the text.

The Crucial Skill: Streaming. You cannot make the user wait 10 seconds for the whole summary. You must use server-sent events to stream the text chunk-by-chunk, making the UI feel alive.

Key Takeaway: The skill here is not "prompt engineering" in isolation. It is managing the state of an asynchronous, non-deterministic AI request and presenting it cleanly to the user.

15.4. The Future: AI Agents and Autonomous Software

From Chatbots to "Do-ers" If 2023-2024 was the era of the "Chatbot" (text-in, text-out), 2025 is the era of the "Agent." This is the cutting edge, championed by research hubs like the Berkeley Center for Responsible, Decentralized Intelligence.

An AI Agent is distinct from a chatbot because it has "agency." It can use tools. It doesn't just tell you the weather; it opens a browser and books a flight based on the weather.

The Anatomy of an Agent Building an agent is a complex JavaScript architectural challenge. It requires a specific loop:

Perceive: The user says, "Book me a hotel in Tokyo for under $200."

Reason (The Brain): The LLM analyzes the request. It realizes it cannot "know" current prices. It decides it needs to use a tool.

Act (Tool Use): The JavaScript runtime executes a function searchHotels(city, price).

Observe: The API returns a JSON list of hotels.

Loop: The LLM reads the JSON and generates a final response to the user.

Design Exercise: The Travel Agent In our updated curriculum, students design this architecture. You define a set of functions—checkWeather(), searchFlights(), bookRoom(). You then implement the logic that allows the LLM to "decide" which function to call and in what order. This is often called "ReAct" (Reasoning and Acting) implementation.

Job Market Implications This moves you from a Senior Developer to a Principal or Architect level. As noted in 2025 job reports, "conversational AI knowledge" is becoming a gatekeeper for leadership roles. You need to understand how to manage "context windows," how to use vector databases for the agent's "memory," and how to prevent the agent from hallucinating or performing dangerous actions.

Key Takeaway: Agents represent the shift from software as a "tool" (Word, Excel) to software as a "partner" that performs work on your behalf.

About Author

Azhar ul Haque Sario is a bestselling author and data scientist with a remarkable record of achievement. This Cambridge alumnus brings a wealth of knowledge to his work, holding an MBA (SZABIST), ACCA (Knowledge Level - FTMS College Malaysia and London College of Accountancy, London), BBA, and several Google certifications, including specializations in Google Data Analytics, Google Digital Marketing & E-commerce, and Google Project Management.

With ten years of business experience, Azhar combines practical expertise with his impressive academic background to craft insightful books. His prolific writing has resulted in an astounding 2810 published titles, earning him the record for the maximum Kindle editions and paperback books published by an individual author in one year, awarded by Asia Books of Records in 2024.

ORCID: https://orcid.org/0009-0004-8629-830X
Azhar.sario@hotmail.co.uk
https://www.linkedin.com/in/azharulhaquesario/

www.ingramcontent.com/pod-product-compliance
Lightning Source LLC
Chambersburg PA
CBHW031347230926
51848CB00002B/423
* 9 7 8 3 3 8 4 7 5 8 8 2 8 *